Figures, Facts, and Fables

Telling Tales in Science and Math

Barbara Lipke

HEINEMANN
Portsmouth, NH

DATE DUE			
GAYLORD			PRINTED IN U.S.A.

Heinemann
A division of Reed Elsevier Inc.
361 Hanover Street
Portsmouth, NH 03801-3912

Offices and agents throughout the world

Excerpt from "Tales from Science" reprinted with permission from NSTA Publications, copyright 1992 from *Science Scope*, National Science Teachers Association, 1840 Wilson Blvd., Arlington, VA 22201-3000.

Library of Congress Cataloging-in-Publication Data
Lipke, Barbara.
    Figures, facts, and fables: telling tales in science and math /
Barbara Lipke.
        p.   cm.
    Includes bibliographical references.
    ISBN 0-435-07105-X
    1. Storytelling.   2. Science—Study and teaching.   3. Mathematics—
Study and teaching.   I. Title.
LB1042.L5   1996
372.64'2—dc20   96-22037
                                                                 CIP

Editor: Leigh Peake
Production: Vicki Kasabian
Cover design: Joni Doherty
Manufacturing: Louise Richardson

Printed in the United States of America on acid-free paper

99 98 97 96 EB 1 2 3 4 5

To my best teachers:
my children—at home and in school

Contents

Acknowledgments

Many people have been involved in the work leading to the publication of this book and I would like to thank them all. In particular, I wish to thank Sheila Enright for her encouragement and the use of her classroom and students, Catherine Conant, Marni Gillard, Naomi Gordon, who started it all, Katie Hereld, Rita Hughes, Emilie Jacobson, Susan Klein, Anne Lewis, Peter and Anne Lipke, Lee Ellen Marvin, Jay O'Callahan who said "Yes! Be a storyteller!" Dr. Patricia Ruane, who issued the challenge, Fred Stein, Jay Sugarman, the Elementary School of New Boston, New Hampshire, and last but not least, Leigh Peake, my editor at Heinemann, for her patience, encouragement, and good humor throughout the process.

Foreword

When Barbara Lipke came to Robert Frost's proverbial fork in the road, she paused, assessed her options, and "chose the one less traveled by." *Figures, Facts, and Fables* is her record of that journey and a road map for those who would follow her storytelling path. The book argues convincingly that storytelling is a vital, powerful, and accessible instructional medium. Story is our primary vehicle for transmitting both content and concepts.

Barbara is trailblazer and navigator. She has widened the roadway, marked it clearly, shored it up where it was weak, added rest stops, and created alternate routes. All this so that you, her fellow traveler, can have safe passage and share the rewards of her discoveries.

Barbara has been in your shoes. She remembers the risk in getting started as a teacher/storyteller, the challenge of becoming a different kind of professional. That is why her approach is so respectful. Barbara makes room for art in progress and for making mistakes. "Stories are forgiving," she teaches. "Stories allow a timid ego to take heart and emerge." With gentle nudges from a firm hand, Barbara guides you onto the path. In a series of well-designed steps and exercises, she debunks the mystery and shares all the tools and skills that she has learned or invented in more than a decade of personal storytelling and teaching. An ancient art form comes alive and becomes possible in these pages.

It is hard to resist Barbara's enthusiasm. Once you understand the terrain and believe in your own potential as storyteller, the world of teaching and learning will transform you and your students. Suddenly, you will make intimate connections. Eye contact will increase dramatically, for as Barbara points out, "There is no book . . . no barrier." Watch the magic take over!

But don't stop here. There is more to learn. Barbara points out fascinating trails where science, math, and storytelling overlap. She invites you to consider the possibilities when "truth and parable [travel] together." For Barbara, stories give information a context where it can be held, considered, and remembered. My personal favorite math-laden story is "Ali Baba and the Forty Thieves." Read the real thing, and you will find a range of modern math skills in practice—everything from arithmetic to estimation, patterning to problem solving, probability to spatial intelligence. Once you begin thinking this way, there is no stopping the connections!

Barbara helps you go with your own flow, for she moves easily between established stories and those she and her students have created. The book includes an annotated bibliography, by subject, as well as a sampler of traditional and original stories. Here are great resources at your fingertips.

Enjoy the total experience of this book, the total immersion of your mind, body, and spirit in the act of storytelling. Mastery of this art is within your grasp and that of your students. I hope to see you on the path, both of us reassured that Barbara Lipke is just ahead, around the bend, brimming with new tales to tell.

Patricia C. Ruane
Superintendent of Schools
Needham, Massachusetts

Preface

Once upon a time I was an elementary school teacher. One year I returned from a sabbatical leave of absence to a "challenging" class. I struggled to teach. I was exhausted at the end of each day.

"Jay O'Callahan is coming tomorrow," my teaching partner said at the end of one particularly trying day.

"What's that?" I asked. I hadn't understood.

"He's a storyteller."

"How long do we have to keep the kids quiet?" I asked.

"It's not like that," he said. I didn't believe him.

The next day we had fifty-two itchy sixth graders sitting on the floor. The door opened and in stepped a tall, gangly man with a prominent Adam's apple, red and white polo shirt, and green chinos.

"Forget this!" I thought.

But I was wrong. For an hour nobody stirred. The students and I stared at the corner of the ceiling where the steam pipes came into the room. We saw firelight dancing on fluted columns. We watched the Green Knight swing his mace at the giant bubble. We tasted "Raspbe-r-r-i-e-s!"

It was a revelation. It was also my introduction to storytelling.

Later, Jay gave a workshop, and I attended. He returned to tell more stories in my classroom. I continued to be entranced.

One day the school librarian said, "Barbara, you should be a storyteller."

"Don't be silly."

She kept after me. "Barbara, I'm not going to nag you anymore. Take a professional day. Go and see Jay. Ask him."

So I did. Jay was most encouraging. I took some courses and I started telling stories. I realized I'd always told stories. I remember once, some years earlier, when I was trying to give my students an idea of what the "climax" of a story was, I told them just a bit of what had happened to me one night when I was alone in the house and I heard a man's heavy footsteps coming up the stairs.

"Who's there?" I yelled. (And I yelled it!) Suddenly the door between my classroom and my partner's flew open. He stuck his head in the door.

"What's wrong?" he demanded, clearly expecting disaster.

"Nothing. I'm just teaching." I was embarrassed.

He retreated to his room. I was rattled.

"What happened?" the kids demanded. They were not embarrassed. Their concentration wasn't disturbed. They wanted to know what happened in my house that night.

There was another time in the early seventies. I had a Cambodian student. The whole school had this family, kindergarten through eighth grade. This boy seemed too old for the sixth grade and I was concerned about him. His math was good but he didn't seem to either read or write. I gave the class a writing assignment. The class bent to the task, pencils moving over clean white paper.

My Cambodian student looked straight ahead. His new pencil, freshly sharpened, lay in the pencil groove.

"Why aren't you writing?" I whispered.

He turned brick red. "I don't know how."

"Tell me your story."

"What story?"

I floundered. "Uh. How you got out of Cambodia."

Very quietly he told me the story of how, one moonless night, long after midnight, his family—perhaps fifty people—gathered silently on the banks of a river and filed onto a raft. He was given an assignment: keep a baby quiet.

The raft was poled soundlessly out onto the dark river and then he failed in his assignment. The baby cried. Search lights went on, machine guns started to chatter. Some of the people on the raft jumped into the water. Some of them could swim. Later, he told me, those who survived gathered on the far side of the river and made their way to Brookline, Massachusetts.

  I was stunned. I sat there, listening. I looked at all the other students working away at their stories. I realized that, no matter how neat and well written those stories were, none would stay with me as powerfully as this simply spoken story.

I began to have a sense of what storytelling was and how I could use it in my teaching—indeed, how I had been using it without realizing what I was doing.

  At first I told my students stories as entertainment—and they were entertained. I began to use stories as I always had, to illustrate ways to develop character or plot. I began to encourage my students to tell stories. I discovered that storytelling was powerful, more powerful than I'd ever imagined, and that it was a way to teach science and math as well as everything else. The storytelling took on a life of its own.

  The first part of this book is the story of that life, the children and the teachers who took the journey with me. The second part is a storytelling teaching unit: practical suggestions to help you use storytelling in your teaching. Appendix A: Stories, consists of seven traditional and original stories to get you started. Appendix B: Resources, is a partially annotated bibliography: books about storytelling and how to do it, and books of stories you can adapt to your classroom needs. Come on in, the water's fine!

Part I

The Journey

"Oh No! Not Another Subject to Teach!" 1

Rationale

I can hear you now. "This is all I need! Another subject in an already impossible curriculum load."

But wait. That's not what storytelling is. Storytelling is not another subject to teach. Storytelling is the oldest and most powerful teaching and learning *method* known.

Storytelling is the way human beings communicate. Not on stage to an audience but to each other, in what we call casual conversation. Listen in the teachers' room. What do you hear? What do you tell? Stories. Anecdotes.

Storytelling has power. It also has a long history. Television is barely fifty years old, radio another twenty. Print is only five hundred years old and writing a mere five thousand. Storytelling has been the way human beings have communicated since they first began to make meaningful sounds. Furthermore, in every culture, the storyteller, often the wise man or shaman, was the keeper of stories, and keeper of the community's knowledge, the person responsible for making sure that every young person learned that knowledge and that one in particular was trained to carry on the custom. The storyteller was the teacher!

Storytelling used to be family custom. To a degree, it still is. Listen around the table at Thanksgiving and you will hear the stories begin to emerge. But the dispersion of families and the advent of radio and television disturbed the custom. For a long time librarians (bless them) were almost the only practitioners of the storytelling art. About twenty-five years ago a groundswell revival began and there are now storytelling events and professional storytellers all across the country. We need to reclaim storytelling as an art and as a teaching method. We need to use it to teach everything, but science and math especially.

"OK. So storytelling is natural and has a history—but storytelling as science and math? You gotta be kidding."

No. I'm not kidding. In fact, one of the most powerful reasons for using storytelling to teach and learn science and math is that it is the natural way to go.

"I managed to skip teaching science again this week!" I once heard a colleague say triumphantly. There was murmured assent and congratulations in the teachers' room.

That declaration came at a time when there had been an article in the newspaper despairing of the fact that only two secondary physics teachers and no math teachers had been certified in the state that year.

I sympathized with the teacher. I was glad that my teaching partner and I traded off our classes: she taught two sections of science, I taught two sections of social studies. I was not comfortable with the idea of teaching science. My husband was a scientist—and one of my sons—and my mother was a physician, but science scared me. My own science education fulfilled the minimum requirements for my high school and college degrees plus one three-hour component in my teaching degree twenty years later. I felt inadequately prepared to teach science!

Over the years, science and math have come to be looked upon as "special." They have gained the reputation of being elitist—too complex and specialized for ordinary people to understand.

The problem is really a two-edged sword. The first edge is the elitist label, in part the responsibility of the scientists and mathematicians themselves. They have allowed themselves to be pictured as very erudite professionals with all the answers to every problem. At the same time, popular culture has depicted them as the "mad scientist" or "crazy mathematician" with wild hair and an absent-minded look. I once heard a science curriculum director advise her teachers to be sure that visiting scientists wore lab coats and used complicated scientific language to impress the students.

The second edge of the sword is our own educational system. Many elementary school teachers feel as inadequate about teaching science as my colleague and I did. They too may have unhappy memories of their science and math education.

But it isn't true that scientists and mathematicians are different. Scientists are people who wonder about things: how they came to be, why they do what they do, and what their properties are. Scientists work by imagining, asking questions, and trying to answer those questions in an organized way. All humans are curious. Curiosity is universal. Why do we stifle that curiosity in ourselves and in our children?

Math is not so different. There are problems everywhere. Human beings are problem solvers. Hand them a problem—a puzzle—and they express a compulsion to solve it that is almost universal. Who among us can walk past the all but completed jigsaw puzzle and resist putting in the last two pieces!

There is an additional problem. Few elementary school teachers majored in science or math and most have had only methods courses: how to teach math and science, not the content. This makes them unsure of what they are teaching and therefore uncomfortable with these subjects. Yet we cannot teach successfully if we are afraid, any more than we can learn if we are afraid.

This book does not deal with subject matter. What it does is to reintroduce a method of teaching science and math that can break the cycle of feeling inadequate. Teaching with storytelling capitalizes on five basic human attributes: curiosity, problem solving, imagination, creativity, and the narrative form. Because stories are a natural way to communicate, science and math lose a lot of their mumbo jumbo and become more accessible, more understandable, more natural. Moreover, storytelling validates those same five attributes in students so they too are freed from fear and encouraged to learn because they are curious and the subject matter is now available. Teachers and students together can approach these subjects with unfettered curiosity and enthusiasm.

We all know that the teacher who teaches her subject with enthusiasm and enjoyment is a good teacher and that the students who approach their learning with eager curiosity will be successful too.

Curiosity and Problem Solving

All children are curious. The four-year-old's ceaseless "Why?" is not merely an attention-getting device, although the harried parent may sometimes feel that it is. The fact of the matter is that the four-year-old needs to know! The world is full of wonderful things to find out about and so she asks, and asks, and asks.

The world is also full of problems to solve, and the first step in problem solving is to ask questions and define the problem. The four-year-old doesn't have to learn this. It is instinctual. We need to encourage our students to ask questions, to define the problems for themselves. Then they will be ready for the next step: solving the problem. This is what scientists and mathematicians do.

We all love to solve problems. We experience a tremendous feeling of satisfaction when we have managed to do that, be it computing a sum, unraveling a knotty social problem, or filling in the last word in the crossword puzzle. That is where the power and the understanding lie. We have all heard the triumphant cry of a child who achieves something new, that cry of affirmation that echoes throughout our lives: "I can do it myself!"

It's the Imagery: Imagination and Creativity

Storytelling creates community. Both the teller and the listeners are engaged in the story. The images each one creates in his mind's eye as the story is told may be different, but all are valid. A storyteller I know says, "The story is the gift the storyteller gives her audience. Each box looks the same, but each one, on opening, contains a unique gift" (Hereld 1993).

I have told a story to thirty children and afterwards asked them to draw their favorite part of the story. I have gotten thirty different pictures, and all of them are right! I believe we are now raising a third generation of children who do not know they have imaginations. All their imagery is imposed by television. They do not know about making pictures in their heads. Imagination is the well-spring of creativity. We need to be sure our students know they have imaginations and know how to use them. We also need to nurture (not stifle) their natural creativity. Storytelling—the teacher's and their own—feeds these needs.

Suppose that all the great scientists and mathematicians had never used their imaginations? Who would have dreamed that there was a cure for rabies or a way to harness the power of particles in an atom? Who would have dreamed there *was* an atom? Where did Euclid get the idea of geometry?

I gave a workshop on storytelling and science to a group of New York City elementary teachers and science specialists. They enjoyed the stories, they asked questions, but in the end one teacher said: "I can see that this is fun and the children would enjoy it. But it's not science. Science is facts, not stories, not imagination."

"Besides," his colleague piped in. "I have to know the answers for my students. I don't know what I'd do if they asked questions I couldn't answer."

The district science coordinator who had sponsored the workshop, said quietly, "But where do you think scientific ideas come from?"

The group was silent.

"They come from imagination, from thinking, from fooling around with ideas."

A stony silence greeted her remarks. It became clear to me that these teachers felt threatened and afraid. As long as they remained fearful, they could not free themselves or their students to discover and create. Storytelling could free them from that fear.

I love the tale of the little boy who heard a story on the radio and then saw the same story on television.

"Which version did you like better?" his mother asked.

"Oh, the radio one, of course."

"Why?"

"Because the pictures were better!"

Human beings thrive on imagination. Too often teaching becomes divorced from imagination, and students find school "b-o-o-o-r-i-n-g !" How often have we heard, or overheard, students say that, and how often have we justified our teaching by telling ourselves that with so much to teach and so many difficult children—or children in difficult circumstances—we "haven't time" for imagination! Storytelling, for teachers and students, is a wonderful way to teach and learn. Storytelling can help in those difficult situations and with those difficult students. The need for stories is as real as the need for food and water. Human beings have a thirst, a hunger, for stories that we may not always recognize.

I told stories in a vocational high school on the Brooklyn-Queens border in New York City. The students came from homes where drugs, alcohol, and violence were everyday realities. They listened avidly. When I had been through the repertoire of stories I thought appropriate for older adolescents, they begged for more so I began to tell the stories I usually reserve for much younger children. They were hungry for those stories too. The storytelling fed their souls and imaginations. They were hungry without knowing what was missing from their lives. Later, I realized that I had been privileged to give them a missing piece of childhood.

People are never too old to listen to stories or to tell stories. I know people in their sixties and seventies who "discover" storytelling. They are as hungry and thirsty, as enthusiastic and bright-eyed, as the five-year-old in the library or the kindergarten classroom.

Storytelling Teaches: Narrative and Memory
Storytelling adds a powerful dimension to teaching. When you tell a story (as opposed to reading it aloud) there is nothing between you and the listeners: no book, no barrier. The imagery and the ideas flow freely back and forth, creating a community of discovery and learning. Storytelling frees teachers and students to use their own imaginations, to create their own narrative voices and tell their own stories. Narrative is the natural way that people communicate. We tell each other stories.

Students respond to stories. They remember information in stories far longer than information they learn from textbooks or lectures. Through some process I do not understand, the information in oral stories imprints itself on our memories. As Kieran Egan has said, "Story is one of the most important human inventions. . . . It is an approach that seeks to tie together memorization and imagination in learning. The story provides the missing link that makes learning meaningful. It evokes, stimulates and develops imagination. . . . Thinking of teaching as storytelling encourages us to think of the curriculum as a collection of the great stories of our culture. Teachers are the tellers of our culture's tales" (Egan 1989).

In 1986 I went to China with a bunch of high school students. Two of them had been my sixth-grade students. Our trip was punctuated with long train rides, and in the course of those rides, as the train moved slowly across the vast countryside, twenty students crowded into the compartment I shared with three other grown-ups and demanded that I tell stories. I retold a story one of my former sixth-graders had heard five years earlier. He allowed himself to be drawn into the story again and listened avidly. At the end he was clearly disturbed.

"What's the matter, John?"

"You changed the story!"

"I did? How?"

"I don't know but it was different." His memory of the story felt sacred to him, and he did not want it changed.

Another time I had a split fourth- and fifth-grade class. In the course of the first year with those students, I told two Native American stories, one in the fall and one in the spring. I kept the fourth graders the next year and in the fall I showed a wonderful Canadian film of a Northwest tribal myth, *The Loon's Necklace*, that used traditional masks. During the discussion that followed, I asked my students what common elements they found in the film (I was thinking of the four directions, wind, mosquitoes, the moon). My former fourth graders came up with small details they remembered from the two stories I had told the previous year, details I had forgotten.

There is a movement to use children's literature to teach math and science. Many teachers, especially those who take the whole language approach to teaching, have embraced the opportunity. Many stories have math and science applications, which help children and teachers see that math and science can be integrated into other subjects—that those subjects need not be discrete and elite. Teachers who integrate children's literature with math and science are already part way on the journey to using storytelling in their math and science teaching.

Self-Esteem: My Children Grow
The real payoff came with the students' performances of their stories for our class, for another class in the school, or for their parents: the growth of their self-esteem. When one child alone legitimately commands an audience and realizes that her story holds people's attention, then the storyteller has found her voice. Stories allow a timid ego to take heart and emerge.

One spring, Irit, a new Israeli child, joined our class. She and her parents arrived one afternoon after the other children had left for the day. She offered me her hand, eyes on the floor. I welcomed her, told her a little about the other children and what we were studying, and showed her where she would sit. I talked briefly with her parents, and when she arrived the next morning, I introduced her to the class. She sat silently at her desk, eyes down, talking to no one, not even to other Israeli children. She came to school on time each morning, sat silently all through the day, and fled as the bell signaled the end of school.

She struggled with her work and was as shy, I learned, with the Hebrew bilingual class as she was with us. Many of the students, especially her compatriots, tried to make friends but their efforts met a silent rebuff.

Her English improved and it was clear that she understood a great deal of what went on in the classroom. I told a story one day and

I could see her concentrate on each word, fully engaged. The next day I called her to my desk.

"Irit," I said, "From now on you have to pay to get into the classroom. Each day you must speak one sentence to me, in English. And it must be a different sentence each day."

She nodded silently.

The next day she paused timidly beside my desk.

"Good morning, Mrs. Lipke. It is a beautiful day." The words were barely breathed.

"Good morning, Irit. You're right. It is a beautiful day."

She fulfilled her entrance fee each day. I had an image of her at home, perhaps with her parents, deciding on her sentence and practicing it. Little by little she began to take part in classroom activities. She made tentative friends with another Israeli girl.

The day I announced that we were all going to become storytellers, I saw Irit shrivel up at her desk and almost disappear under the carpet. At the end of the day, she fled, her eyes brimming with tears.

The next morning Irit's sentence was a desperate question: "Do I have to tell a story, Mrs. Lipke?"

"Of course. Everyone will. You'll see. It'll be fun."

"Couldn't I just write the story?"

Two sentences!

"No, Irit. I'll make it easy and safe, I promise. You'll see."

The storytelling unit takes about a month and it starts with little steps, one activity at a time, in which everyone participates. Irit was very cooperative. She decided on a story and chose her Israeli friend as a working partner. She worked earnestly on her story. The day she told it to me, we sat knee to knee and she spoke so softly I had trouble hearing her. When she told her story to the whole class, they burst into applause and cheered her performance. She blushed and smiled. The evening we invited all the parents to come, it was Irit who asked me if she could tell her story to a room full of strangers. She had found her voice!

My Storytelling Expands

Storytelling began to spill over from entertainment into language arts skills. Because my students and I were having so much fun with the stories, I began to teach them to be storytellers. Most of them took to it like ducks to water.

In the beginning, each of us decided what kind of story we wanted to tell. Jim chose to tell his favorite book from when he was little. Jim's love of that book shone through his simple telling. His listeners came to love the little red ball story as much as he did. Nora told an original story about finding a mythical pony in a meadow and flying away on it. Other students chose familiar folk and fairy tales or younger children's books from the library. I found myself creating a story about a girl who discovered the self-confidence she needed to play baseball through the intervention of space creatures. My inspiration for that story came from a wonderful book by Chris van Allsburg called *The Mysteries of Harris Burdick*. It's a book of pictures with captions that challenges the reader to think creatively.

We were having a ball. I discovered that my students' reading and writing improved. They were reading a lot, even my reluctant readers. Some of them read a dozen or more stories to find one they wanted to tell. And they were reading for a purpose! It was different from the kind of reading they had done before.

They began to be concerned about the characters in their stories. How could they portray a wicked witch? What words, what imagery, would help the listener see and hear how evil she was? Their vocabularies grew richer. They searched for the right words to describe settings and characters, to create mood. They went further and searched for voices and physical stances to fit their characters. Their stories took hold of them, took on lives of their own.

Not all of them, of course. There were students whose stories didn't "take off," but even they were enjoying the process so much that they worked hard and made gains in their own ways.

Further Discoveries

It occurred to me that in my Ancient Civilizations Social Studies curriculum I could tell myths. The Greek and Roman myths were familiar and easily available. The Sumerian and Egyptian ones were more elusive, but I found them in Samuel Noah Kramer's *History Begins at Sumer* and Roger Lancelyn Green's *Tales of Ancient Egypt* (see Appendix B). In a way, I felt they were more fun for me to tell, more challenging but safer because I felt I could tell them in my own way. It took me a long time to realize that my own way of telling any story was the right way for me to tell it.

I experimented. I tried telling stories in history. The students perked up and listened. The next step was to invite my students to tell stories as a way of reporting to the rest of the class on the independent research projects they undertook. They researched the information for their stories and, with their listeners, internalized it.

And Opportunities

My use of storytelling widened. My school system tried a new approach to staff development. They created a one day a week grant called "Teacher as . . ." designed to encourage professional development for the classroom teacher without leaving teaching. There were four such positions available. I became Teacher as Storyteller. One day each week I left my classroom in the capable hands of a substitute teacher who wanted to work part-time, and taught storytelling to teachers and students in all eight Brookline elementary schools.

In each school I worked with four classes for four weeks. I worked with a variety of grade levels and special classes. The special classes included prekindergarten, English as a Second Language, Bilingual, and .4 Special Education. This latter class included eleven- to fifteen-year-olds who were challenged in many ways. Each class taught me new things about the power and efficacy of storytelling, and about how to teach kids and teachers to be storytellers.

One of the first things I learned was how to engage teachers. I had many more requests for my program than I could fit into my schedule, so I was able to pick and choose. I asked these teachers to teach storytelling during the four-week period I visited their classrooms, and I asked each of them to stay in the classroom and model "teacher as student" while I was teaching. This arrangement had a number of advantages:

1. The teacher had an opportunity to become a student and see teaching from the students' point of view.

2. The teacher had the opportunity to observe the lesson and modify it to fit her class, her style, and her needs.

3. The teacher was learning in her own classroom at a time when teaching was her first priority, not after school or on a Saturday when she was exhausted or had other things to do.

4. The teacher's presence made my job easier because she knew her class and handled any discipline problems.

5. The students saw that the teacher was learning too. The message they got was "This is important. The teacher is doing it!"

There were very few disruptive moments. I remember only one. The regular teacher had become ill and had had to leave. The substitute was brand new and on her very first assignment. It was hard to tell who was more insecure, the students, the substitute, or me! But over time, the substitute teacher found that the storytelling unit gave her a handle on a difficult situation, and the class responded. They enjoyed telling stories and used the opportunity to work out some of their problems.

Each week I held pre- and postvisit conferences with the teachers. I cheered them on, and all the students I worked with became storytellers. In each class, the teacher chose the focus of the storytelling. Sometimes it was folktales or fairy tales. Once it was U.S. presidents. In one second grade it was original animal stories. At the end of that school year, an administrator challenged me to find a way to use storytelling to teach science. I thought I did that already, but I had a lot to learn. (The full story is told in Chapter 3.)

After experimenting with storytelling in teaching science, the next logical step was to see if math and storytelling were a good fit. I had seen work in mathematics and children's literature. Several people I knew—storytellers and teachers—were beginning to think about storytelling and math. I did too. I read. I thought. I researched. I borrowed students and tried out a number of ideas.

I started with a suburban fourth grade, moved on to a rural fourth grade, to younger children, and to an advanced seventh-grade math class. Although I sometimes used the same story, "King Kaid of India," a traditional tale (see Chapter 4), and sometimes very different stories, both students and teachers responded to the idea of math and storytelling with amazement and enthusiasm.

A first-grade teacher looked on skeptically and then stood astounded as her students helped me tell "Goldilocks and the Three Bears." They found more than a dozen math problems in the story and got involved in writing out the problems and solving them together. When they were asked what they had learned from the storytelling and math exercise there was universal agreement among the students. Although they expressed it in different ways, all of them said that storytelling made math fun, and they could see that math was everywhere if you did "math thinking"!

Teachers *Can* Tell Stories

True, the term "storyteller" can sound scary.

"I couldn't do that. Stand up in front of an audience and tell stories."

But if you are a teacher, you already do. Mark Wagler, a storyteller-turned-teacher says, "Teaching is a performing art!" And what better place to try a new kind of performance than that nice, safe place, your own classroom, where you know the students and they know you!

"Not me. It's too scary," I can hear you saying.

It really isn't. Have you ever told your students about the time you . . . You have? Oh, so you have told stories in your classroom!

"Well, sort of. But how do I begin to be a storyteller?"

There are a number of ways. Storytelling has been experiencing a renaissance. In many parts of the country you will find storytellers who give courses independently or as part of college offerings. You can take courses or workshops in storytelling. Or, find a colleague you enjoy working with and enlist her in your scheme. Use "Teaching Storytelling," the second part of this book, as a guide. Work together and support each other. Or, as the kids say, "Just do it!" Tell a favorite story you remember—or tell a story to illustrate a point you want to teach. Practice a couple of times and then tell it to your class. Keep it short and simple. Don't memorize it. Know the sequence and the characters. Your first story may be only two or three minutes long—just long enough to get from the beginning to the end.

Stories are forgiving. As long as you know why you are telling it, the story will work. And it will probably change each time you tell it. Stories grow in depth and understanding, though not necessarily in length.

"But suppose I make a mistake?"

Who will know?

A professional storyteller I know says, "Oh, and did I remember to tell you that on her way to her grandmother's house, Little Red Riding Hood met a wolf?"

There is no wrong way to tell a story. Each teller does it in her own style.

Do you remember when you were a student teacher and tried to teach "just like your cooperating teacher"? In time, you got your own classroom, survived that difficult first year, and little by little developed your own teaching style. Storytelling is a bit like that. Each teller develops her own way of telling a story, and for that person, it's the best way: the most comfortable, the most fun, the most effective. Your students will find a whole new outlook on school and learning.

My colleague Jeanette taught seventh- and eighth-grade science. She loved stories and storytelling but always insisted that *she* couldn't tell stories. I nagged her gently. She took part in afterschool workshops where I taught teachers basic storytelling techniques. One day she stopped me in the hall. Her face was flushed and her eyes sparkled.

"I told a story about chemical reactions! The kids loved it! Even Charles listened and understood!" Charles had been the scourge of every teacher from kindergarten to seventh grade.

Marilyn, a student in my class, made her own discoveries. She was having trouble remembering the parts of a tree cross section and failed the standard end-of-unit test. The make-up test asked her to "Write a story using all the information you learned in the Tree Unit." When I read Marilyn's test, I discovered that she had made the parts of the tree trunk into characters in her story. Her cambium layer was an adolescent boy, forever eating and growing. She even had a part in which the sapwood became the tough guy and changed to heartwood. The story allowed her to remember and use the scientific facts.

How to Tell Stories

In her book *In The Middle*, Nancie Atwell says you need three things to write: a subject, time, and response. For storytelling, I add a fourth: safety. "You can't learn if you're not safe" (Wagler 1994). Just as there are different kinds of stories to tell and different styles of storytelling, there are different approaches to learning to tell stories.

"Teaching Storytelling," the second part of this book, goes through the process step-by-step. Here is a brief summary:

Choose a story you like, one you feel you can "get into." Read it through several times. Sketch a few of the scenes in color. Think about smells, tastes, textures, and sounds as they become apparent to you. Figure out who the characters are and how they got to be that way. Jot down some phrases that help create the mood and imagery you experience in the story.

Don't memorize your story. What? *Don't memorize your story.* Why? Because memorization is a crutch. If you have memorized your story and you forget, you'll be sunk. Furthermore, the images you create will be images of the printed page and, believe it or not, your audience will also see the printed page. Learn the sequence. Know the story in your gut, but not in your head.

Take a break. Go for a jog or bake some cookies.

Try telling the story to yourself. Some people like to tape themselves and listen to the tape, while others are uncomfortable taping and listening. Tell the story to a good friend. Ask her to listen and tell you (choose a response that is specific but is not threatening) whether there is any place that's confusing, whether she can tell who's talking, or whether she can see where the story takes place.

Ask for a specific response (just one) before you tell your story. Ask your listener to start by telling you, specifically, what worked well in the story. Be sure you keep control of your story. If your listener has a suggestion that feels comfortable and helpful, incorporate it. If the suggestion grates for any reason, ignore it.

Think about the story before you go to sleep or as you brush your teeth. Then take a deep breath and tell it to your class. They'll love it. If you tell them it's your first try, they'll love it even more. If part of your purpose is to get them telling stories, they'll welcome the idea that you will be learning with them. I've always believed that the best teaching is modeling. Learning to tell stories as you teach storytelling is a powerful way to go. When you become a storyteller you gain a powerful new teaching tool. Go for it!

Students As Storytellers

How about student storytellers? Yes. By all means, turn your students into storytellers. It's a great way to learn. The information they *tell* in stories will become internalized. After all, they too are natural storytellers. How about all the wonderful tales they tell as excuses for tardiness or uncompleted homework? "The dog ate my homework" is more than a funny cliche, it's a natural.

In teaching students to tell stories, we teach all the language skills, especially the ones that come first developmentally but are often neglected in school, listening and speaking. Elocution may be long gone from most curricula, but here is real motivation for learning to speak clearly and listen carefully.

The techniques I use to teach students storytelling are modeled on a writing process approach. Students work in pairs, in small groups, and then with the whole class to develop their stories, to practice, and to get a response. It is a cooperative learning process; students help each other.

Just as you want to feel safe when you tell stories, so do your students. I take my students step by step, a little bit at a time, into storytelling and performance. I usually begin with a game of Telephone or Pass the Message. You remember Telephone, when someone in the circle whispers a message and you have to get that message, unchanged, all the way around the circle? Why Telephone? There are several reasons. First, it sharpens both listening and speaking skills. In order to understand and repeat the message everyone has to listen carefully and speak clearly. I know, children sometimes deliberately sabotage the message, but if you keep the message very simple, "Once upon a time," for example, and tell the students (as I have) that forty-seven sixth graders got the message around unchanged, you challenge them to meet that record! Second, it's nonthreatening. No one is center stage and no one has to perform. Third, everyone takes part.

There are other nonthreatening games that include everyone: Pass the (Imaginary) Ball, Change the Object, charades, mirrors, and, more specific to storytelling, Fortunately, Unfortunately and Point of View. (These are described in the second part of this book.) I start each day's storytelling session with one or two games. As I teach the unit, I too work on a story. Students welcome the teacher to the story-learning process. They want to hear my story—and yours.

Discourage your students from writing their stories down. Why? There are a number of reasons. Students tend to feel that once something is written it is carved in stone, and they will memorize (see above). Second, they will do a lot of other writing as they work out the details of their story: characterizations, settings, sequence, special imagery. Third, a told story is crafted differently from a written story. Fourth, a whole population of students are "turned off" by having to write everything down—because it's not the way they learn, because writing has always spelled "failure" for them, because the written language is not yet available to them, or for some other reason. These are the students for whom storytelling, *precisely because it is oral and not written*, may provide a bridge to success.

I have developed a set of "rules" that help make the classroom a safe place to take risks. If they have a familiar ring, it is because we have walked through them already.

1. The story belongs to the storyteller.

2. The storyteller decides what (specific) response she wants in this telling.

3. The listener tells the storyteller specifically what worked well in this telling and then responds specifically to the storyteller's request.

4. The storyteller listens to the response and decides whether to use any of the suggestions.

5. The story belongs to the storyteller.

What responses? With your class, brainstorm a list of possible responses, things that might be useful to know as they work on their stories. You could prepare the list yourself and post it, but if the students know the responses are their own, they will own them and be motivated to use them. Response requests do something more. They not only keep the storyteller in charge of her own story, they also focus the listener. The listener has a specific task.

Students change partners, move from one-on-one to small groups, and finally tell their story to the whole class. Telling a story to the whole class is more akin to a dress rehearsal than a performance, but as in the writing process when the final draft of a story is read, at the whole class telling there is only positive response. If the storyteller wants specific response, she may ask for it. I always tell storytellers that the story will change, that unlike written stories, there is no final version. Each time the story is told, it will probably be a little different. With each telling, the storyteller learns more about herself and more about the story. The story grows in depth and understanding as the storyteller grows!

Performance is probably for a different audience: another class, a group in the library, parents, clients in a nursing home, listeners to local radio or community-access television. Your students will have worked long and hard on their stories and they deserve the opportunity to tell them to different audiences.

As students become storytellers, a whole new world will open to them. Their language skills will grow—and their self-esteem will grow too. They will discover other uses for storytelling, both in and out of school. Their use of curiosity, imagination, creativity, narrative, and problem solving will be validated. What a gift for you and for them.

"How Can I Tell My Principal We're Not Just Having Fun?"

2

There are people around the education business who want to know the pedagogical value of everything you do as a teacher. If you and your class are having so much fun, your principal or district supervisor may ask (and you may well ask too) why you should spend your precious teaching time on anything as frivolous as storytelling. Here are some of the reasons:

Storytelling Motivates Students
Storytelling is fun and engaging. Students who usually talk, write notes, or bother others suddenly become attentive.

A new student, Joe, arrived in my class one spring from New York City. Every time I looked at him he said, "I din' do nuttin!'" Once, bringing the class upstairs from the computer lab for that useless twelve minutes before lunch, I told them that if they got upstairs and into their seats quietly, I'd tell a story.

"If we're good li'l kiddies, she'll tell us a story," Joe mocked. I recognized the common belief that stories and storytelling are only for little kids. My other students knew better. They turned on him in a flash:

"Be quiet!"

"It's special. You'll see!"

He did see and became a staunch fan—and practitioner of storytelling. He was the first to shush others if anyone interrupted a story!

Storytelling gets students' attention as listeners and as tellers.

Listening to stories draws students in and intrigues them. Their listening has a different quality; it is focused. When students tell stories they are focused in a different way: to do their best, to engage others, *to tell their story*. They are motivated to improve many skills and to gain mastery of specific subject matter.

Skills Gained in Communication/Language Arts

No matter what the subject matter, every student has a basic educational need: the ability to communicate. That means each student needs the skills to be a good listener and an articulate speaker, to write, and to read. With storytelling, students show marked gains in communications skills. The language arts are the basis of communication and a foundation of elementary teaching.

Listening and Speaking

Language arts is the first skills area that comes to mind when we think of storytelling. And the first language arts, developmentally, are listening and speaking. A baby learns to listen first of all. He learns to listen for his mother's voice, and then he learns to listen for her tone. I have seen a two-week-old baby become stiff, tense his back, and start to cry when his parents squabbled, and relax at the soothing endearments that followed. He learns language, both comprehension and use, by imitation. Storytelling addresses both of these skills.

Listening is seldom taught in today's curriculum, and students listen less and less. They hear, but what they hear and how they interpret it may be more influenced by the sounds of radio and television flowing past their ears than by any need to listen in an active way. But children do listen actively to stories. They want to hear what happens. Watch any group of students listening to a storyteller and you will see focused listening. The slack-jawed look that accompanies most TV watching is absent. Listening clearly has a purpose.

As for speaking, the teaching of elocution has gone the way of the great auk, but storytelling is a wonderful teacher of clear speech. Why? Because when students tell stories, it is important to them that their listeners comprehend what they are saying. They work hard to make sure that they are understood.

One year Ivan joined my class. He had recently immigrated from the Soviet Union. His English was heavily accented, almost incomprehensible until we became accustomed to it, and his English vocabulary was sparse, but he had a story he wanted to tell. He told a story about his great-grandfather as he left his carpenter's shed in the forest late one winter evening to return home. He carried his toolbox because he had a job to do at home.

As he started out he heard something moving in the brush beside the path. All he could see was a huge dark shadow, and then he heard a low rumbling growl. He reached into his toolbox, grabbed a heavy hammer, and threw it at the shadow. There was a surprised grunt and the shadow moved quickly away. Ivan's great-grandfather had frightened off an enormous bear! The story was brief (perhaps three minutes) but in that three minutes Ivan had us all on the edge of our seats. He struggled with his English but he made sure we all understood his story.

Literature

Storytelling is a fine way to introduce students to literature. It is the most obvious use there is. Librarians have always told stories. Why not just read the book? Reading aloud is also a wonderful way to introduce literature. Everyone should read aloud and everyone should be read to. I read aloud to my own children and to my students every day. But storytelling is different. When someone tells a story, there is nothing between the listeners and the teller—no intermediary, no book, only the teller, the tale, and the listeners. The energy flows back and forth. We are all there together, sharing the experience, forming a community. The fact that a child can then go and find more of that story or other stories in a book is an added inducement to read and to share the reading. So use storytelling to introduce your students to literature. Pick a piece of a book you particularly enjoy and tell it without the book. If it's a book you've been reading aloud to your class year after year, it's easy. Just put the book aside—you probably hardly use it anyway—and tell your favorite part.

A friend of mine who regularly taught the novel *Tom Sawyer* got so involved in the funeral scene she was telling the story. The book was open but she wasn't using it at all. Her department head wandered into the room with a visitor during the "nonreading," and they were quickly as enthralled as the students. Afterwards the department head said, "That was extraordinary! You had us all there in the church balcony with Tom! That scene really came to life!"

Reading

Which leads me directly to storytelling and reading. We are rapidly becoming a nation of nonreaders. The last year I taught in my own fifth-grade classroom, I had two very bright children who did not read.

They could decode. They knew their phonics. They knew the words, but they didn't seem to take any meaning from what they read.

One day I was working with William. He was reading out loud to me, and when I stopped him and asked him what he had read, he didn't know.

"I read much better when I read to myself," he explained.

"We all do," I said. "Read to yourself."

After a few minutes I again asked what he had read.

He stammered and hemmed and hawed. He clearly didn't know. I had a sudden flash of insight.

"William, do you read the way you watch TV?"

"Yeah. Sure . . . What do you mean?"

"When you watch TV, do you just sit and watch the pictures go by?"

"Yeah. Sure."

"And when you read, do you just let the words go by?"

"Yeah. Sure."

"William," I said, "that's not reading."

"Huh?"

We sat and talked during the time he came for extra help before school in the morning.

"The author of that book," I explained, "has a story to tell you. Instead of telling it out loud, the way I sometimes do, he has written it down for you to read and understand."

"I like your stories," William said.

"I'm glad you do, but I want you to be able to know about all kinds of stories, not just the few I know and tell. Books are full of stories and if you can read, you can enjoy all those stories too."

William was dubious. The reading specialist and I put our heads together and tried to figure out what would help him become a reader. Clearly he understood stories when I told them, and when someone read aloud to him—at least, he understood the concept that books had meaning. It felt like a breakthrough, or at least an explanation of why this bright boy was not reading.

The other child who did not read was Mary. There were problems at home but that didn't seem to be it. I asked her the same questions I had asked William and got the same answers. Mary was quicker to see the connection than William and soon was really reading. She figured out that if she read, it should mean something. If the story was an exciting one, she got "hooked" and had no trouble at all. If the book was one that did not interest her, she soon reverted to her old habit of letting the words go by. It took time and practice and concentrated effort on her part to read those "boring" books, but she did finally "get it"!

At eighth-grade graduation, William won the school's most prestigious prize for best all-around student. He, too, had finally gotten the message!

Something else happened with reading. If students were looking for stories they might want to tell, they read differently. When I assigned folktales as the focus of class storytelling, the librarian put her collections on reserve for my class. Suddenly, even reluctant readers were reading ten or more folktales to find one they really wanted to tell. The reading they were doing had a different tone than when they read Judy Blume books, or Sweet Valley High books, or other fiction they had chosen or I had assigned. They were reading for a purpose and they knew what that purpose was. At the same time, they were talking about the stories and recommending particular stories or books to each other. When the stories were told, we compared how a teller told a story to how other students remembered it from their reading. They came to appreciate the teller's changes and characterizations.

Writing

Writing changed too. When I teach storytelling, as I have mentioned, I try to discourage my students (of any age) from writing the story down. Stories for telling can and should change as the teller and his experience change and grow! Revision is in the telling and retelling.

How does storytelling affect student writing? Didn't you just say you discouraged students from writing down their stories? Yes, I did. But there is other writing to do when you are developing or learning a story. Students needed to learn about the characters in their stories. My students used a variety of methods. They wrote character studies. Sometimes they developed a whole family and career for a character. There were students, of course, who claimed that their character was an orphan with no family at all, no friends, and no interests. I didn't let them get away with that! Sometimes they used charts (see "Teaching Storytelling") or drew pictures. Sometimes, in talking to a rehearsal partner, they fleshed out their characters, learning more about them and giving them greater depth. What they learned—that they had to have real, believable characters in the stories they told—transferred to written stories.

Their sense of dialogue was sharpened. They listened to their own talk, to each other's stories, and to tapes of professional storytellers. They listened when we had visiting storytellers. They became more aware of how people speak. They could hear the difference between real speech and stilted speech. That transferred too.

The same thing was true when they worked on setting. They drew pictures. They listened while I took them on guided imagery journeys. They learned that setting includes colors, sounds, smells, tastes, and tactile components. Their vocabularies grew as they searched for just the right word or phrase to create the images they saw in their own heads as they told their story.

They learned about plot. Many of the elementary students I taught wrote "bed-to-bed" stories: "I woke up and heard mother moving around in the kitchen. I could smell the bacon frying . . ." Every detail of dressing, eating, walking to school, each subject in school, each interchange on the playground, each step of the walk home was carefully recorded. "As I walked up the steps to my apartment a fire-breathing dragon roared at me!"

As they told stories, they began to realize where the story was and what made a story. This also transferred to their written fiction.

They even achieved a heightened sense of sentence structure!

I don't claim that all these wonderful things happened for every student. They didn't. But there was overall improvement in all these areas, and it seemed painless. Storytelling accomplished what workbooks and grammar lessons barely touched.

Storytelling Teaches Questioning

When kids are motivated and intrigued, they ask questions. They want to know more. When their imaginations are engaged, the questions become broader, deeper, more creative. We need to recognize the importance of asking questions. Isn't that how learning occurs? When we encourage students' questions, aren't we encouraging that basic human instinct, curiosity? Asking questions is an important skill. We learn by being curious, by asking. When you ask your students, "What else do you want to know about that story?" you encourage that curiosity. Isn't questioning what scientists and mathematicians do? When students ask questions everyone learns, including the teacher. A former colleague used to tell his students, "There are no dumb questions. The chances are that the question you ask, five other kids want answered but aren't brave enough to ask."

Storytelling Teaches How to Pose Problems

Asking questions leads to posing problems. All stories pose problems—and provide solutions.

When students raise questions, they can easily be encouraged to take the next steps: to refine the questions, pose the problems, hypothesize the solutions, test the hypotheses . . .

Wait a minute. What's going on here? Yes, it's true. Read Chapter 3. When you use storytelling to teach and learn, you will find it has many applications and those applications encompass sound pedagogy.

Storytelling Helps Students Learn

The more I thought of ways to teach with storytelling, the more connections I saw between teaching/learning and storytelling. One day I had just finished teaching a lesson on how to read tree rings. We had a cross section of a tree and practiced reading it. We'd talked about what the different marks on the cross section meant. I wanted to know whether my students had understood the lesson.

"You have three minutes," I said. "Turn to your neighbor and tell her or him a story based on what you've just learned. You can be anything you want: an insect, a tree, a sidewalk, a scientist, a woodcutter."

I waited. I walked around and eavesdropped. At the end of four minutes I had the students switch: tellers became listeners and a new set of stories were created. We took time and shared some of the stories. Susan told a story about a carpenter ant in dire straits because it had eaten all the rotten wood within reach and was stuck by its waist, unable to go backward or forward. Mark told his story from the point of view of a vain tree ring who bemoaned the fact that it would bear the scar of a lightning strike forever. Some of the students chose to write and illustrate their stories. Some taped them and some told them to younger brothers and sisters at home. Some felt that their stories weren't worth preserving, and that was all right too. But all the students remembered a great deal about how to read tree rings! Telling the stories, even on a very informal, spur-of-the-moment basis, helped the students internalize the information. The stories they created and told fixed the information in a context. It was now theirs.

Stories as Evaluation

The next logical step was to use storytelling—or at least story—to find out what my students knew, that is, to assess their knowledge.

At the end of a science unit, I gave a traditional short answer/essay unit test. Some students did not do well. They asked for a make-up test and took it along with a couple of students who had been absent for the first test. My question for them was simple: "Write a story that includes all the information you can recall from the unit." The tests I took home to correct were a revelation. There was more information in those stories than there had been in the "formal" test I had given earlier. Here was further evidence that story is a natural and powerful way to learn. What an addition to both student and teacher portfolios!

Storytelling to Report on Individual Projects

More pedagogy? Absolutely. Do your students do individual and/or small group research in science? in math? in other subjects? And do you have them share that information with the rest of the class? Or at a science or math fair? Do you, as I did, encourage many ways to report? On this particular occasion, it happened that we were coming to the end of a long social studies unit on the Civil War. The students had completed individual research projects and were presenting their projects to the rest of the class. There were lifelines and battle boards, murals, campaign maps, charts, dioramas, mobiles, and coffee-stained diaries with the edges carefully burned. Every one was furiously taking notes; there was going to be a test on the unit.

"Slow down!" someone called.

"How do you spell *Shiloh*?"

"Mrs. Lipke, do we have to know all the states that seceded?"

"Which side was Stonewall Jackson on?"

I watched and wondered. What would these students take away from their three months' study? They were so bogged down in details. Would they have any sense of the overall picture?

Kathy had chosen storytelling to present her research. She walked slowly to the front of the room and leaned against the chalkboard.

"You can put your pencils away," she said apologetically. "There's no information in this story. In fact, I don't even know why I'm standing here." She looked at me. "Do I have to?"

I nodded and smiled in what I hoped was an encouraging way.

She sighed, and faced the class, still leaning against the chalkboard.

Her subject was the Ku Klux Klan. She looked pained. She began her story.

She told her story in the first person as a young freed black man, after federal troops were withdrawn from the south. He was determined that his children get an education and each night he crept into the white school and copied whatever was on the board onto a scrap of paper or a piece of wood. He was seen and the men dressed in white sheets rode, burned his crops, and warned him not to return.

Kathy was no longer leaning against the blackboard. She was no longer in the classroom. She had become her hero. She felt the hot, moist night air of the Georgia swamps. She heard the mosquitoes whine. I glanced at my class. They were there with her. No one stirred. They too heard the mosquitoes. They heard the fearsome hoofbeats of horses. The man's wife and children begged him not to go back to the school but he was stubborn. He crept back and the next time the Klan rode they burned his crops and his house, and shot one of his children.

Kathy ended her story, speaking as a surviving child, looking up at her father: "Daddy, why do they hate us?"

When she finished no one stirred. We were all still there, watching, hearing, understanding. Kathy slunk back to her seat, convinced that the whole thing was a failure, that she had made a fool of herself.

Then the class returned to the world of the classroom and burst out in long, sustained applause; not the polite applause fifth graders usually give their classmates but the stunned response of a truly moved audience.

Later, in the end-of-unit test, there was a choice of essay questions. More than ninety percent of the class wrote on the Ku Klux Klan. There was no question that they understood terrorism, what it meant, and how it worked. Later, when I told Kathy, she was astounded.

"Me?" she asked. "I did that?"

Students Keep Track of Their Learning

Learning logs are useful in many subjects, and storytelling is no exception. Marni (Schwartz) Gillard introduced me to learning logs with her student storytellers. They sounded like a good idea to me, and I tried them in my classroom.

In their logs, students documented their storytelling progress. They kept a list of resources they consulted, they noted what they had done during that day's storytelling period, and they reported on what they had observed about other students' rehearsals. The notebooks became a further resource for them and for me. I checked them regularly and sometimes found that one student had solved a problem another student was struggling with. "Talk to Mike," I wrote one night in Sam's log. "He found a way to work this out last week. Maybe he can help you."

If we empower students to keep track of their own progress, they are motivated to keep going. If they identify where they are, they can figure out where they need to go next. Being in charge is a powerful motivator for progress.

All these ways of using storytelling have applications for teaching science and math as well as other subjects. New approaches often provide fresh incentives and more effective and exciting teaching.

Storytelling Helps with Many Populations

Most teachers today deal with many populations: children whose first language is not English, children with special needs, children who come from less than ideal home settings, and homeless children.

English as a Second Language

The year I was Teacher as Storyteller in Brookline, I worked with all sorts of classes. One day I found myself in a seventh- and eighth-grade ESL class. There were eight students and seven languages: Russian, Hebrew, Korean, Chinese, Japanese, Spanish, and Iranian. I had spoken with the teacher, and she had assured me that these students were beginning to have some fluency in English. I discovered that "beginning" and "some" were the operative words.

I told them "The Tailor," a story known in many versions and many countries. It is the ultimate recycling story. A tailor makes himself a coat and when it begins to wear out, he turns it into a jacket, a vest, a cap, a button, and finally, "there is just enough left to make this story!" (see Appendix A).

The response to the story was gratifying. About half the students knew a version from their own country.

"I've told you a story," I said, "and now I'd like each of you to tell me a story, a different story than the one I told. Tell it first in your own language and then tell it to us in English."

There were a few feeble protests and then one of the Israeli boys began. The story was brief and his Hebrew fluent. His struggle to tell the story in English was apparent but successful. Seven other stories followed. The stories were traditional tales from each country, and the students' delight and ease of telling them in their native language made it clear that storytelling was not something new to them. What was astonishing to me was that three of those stories turned out to be different versions of the same story.

Each student heard the music of a different first language. Each one recognized how difficult it was to tell the story in English. They felt a bond of kinship. The stories, the music of the different languages, and the struggle to tell the stories in English built bridges of understanding for these students from all corners of the world.

Special Needs

That same year I learned about students with special needs. I had, over the years, documented the behavior and academic struggles of students who clearly needed extra help, and I knew there were special classes that served students like these. I had visited those classrooms as an observer. Now I was a guest teacher, working with a colleague, their regular teacher.

The class was a .4 Special Education class designed to serve the most severely challenged students in the system. These were older students, chronologically aged eleven to fifteen, who had multiple handicaps. All tested low IQ, and some had physical difficulties as well. I tried to imagine how storytelling would work for these children. They clearly enjoyed the stories I told them. Would they be able to tell stories? They had never performed. What would happen?

I worked with their teacher, a remarkable woman, who taught me as well as her students. They too were remarkable. They had stories to tell, and tell them they did! Even George, whose challenges were the most severe—cleft palate, developmentally delayed, confined to crutches, and with severe auditory and visual deficits—wanted to tell the story of the Exodus. "An Mo es sai, 'Yet my pe o ho!'" His crutches supported him as he flung his arms wide. He was Moses! He told the story with such passion that we all saw the parting of the waters of the Red Sea and saw the children of Israel escape Pharaoh's pursuing army.

Janise, a pretty, delayed girl of eleven, told a one-minute story that broke my heart, because it let us know how alone she was, how other children in school and in her neighborhood rejected her.

Each student in the class used the opportunity to tell a story. One boy told a story about his family, where alcohol and violence were part of everyday life. A girl told her version of "Little Red Riding Hood." Several students retold the plots of television shows. Yet, for each student, storytelling provided a first opportunity to perform for an audience, to command attention in a legitimate way, even if only for a minute or two.

It was a first step. When I moved on after my four once-a-week visits, the teacher and students went on telling stories: stories that enhanced listening and speaking skills, introduced literature, expanded vocabularies, and built much needed self-confidence.

Multicultural Applications

Multicultural curricula represent an effort to have children understand more about the many cultures and beliefs whose strands make up the rich tapestry of our country and the world. I know of two principal resources for multicultural storytelling: folktales and family histories. Folktales are a wonderful resource, but be careful when you choose to tell a folktale from another culture. Often, in translation, the frame is changed to fit the one we find comfortable and familiar: "Once upon a time . . . happily ever after." If you can read these stories in direct translation, or translated by someone steeped in the native culture, you may find that they don't seem to end comfortably, that the moral of the story is missing or seems strange. Beliefs are different in different cultures, and understanding this is the essence of multicultural studies. This kind of difference is fairly easy to find in Native American stories. Another excellent place is Virginia Hamilton's *In the Beginning: Creation Stories from Around the World*.

The other multicultural resource, one that most teachers have right in the classroom, is their students. My fifth grade in Brookline represented seventeen different first- or second-generation countries of origin. I made immigration part of our American history study and sent my students home to research their family histories. I was careful to emphasize that we were not looking for family trees, but for family stories, the kind that get told around the table at Thanksgiving.

I taught the students how to interview. I asked them to make appointments, to say "please" and "thank you." We talked about who to interview and brainstormed questions to ask at home. We role played the interviews, and when they interviewed me, I gave one-word responses to some of the questions they asked:

"Were you ever scared?"

"Yes."

We talked about the importance of follow-up. "Tell me about that, please." "What happened then?" "What else?" "And then . . . ?"

The technique of coming up with further questions is one most children have to learn. It does not come naturally.

I also wrote a letter to send home, with a tear-off sheet so I was sure parents knew what was going on. (You will find that letter in "Teaching Storytelling.") I urged students to search through attics and storage rooms, go through family pictures with the person they were interviewing, and get as much information as they could. Some students taped their interviews and some took notes. They went back and did follow-up interviews in many cases because there was more information they needed to know. They ended up writing their family histories, and each student chose one incident to tell as a story.

But first we sat in a circle and told "about" our stories—one sentence, less than a minute. Everyone shared; no one was center stage performing. This helps make sure storytellers feel safe about telling stories: one small step at a time.

"My story is about the time I ran away from home when I was two."

"My story is about a time when my mother got blamed for something her brother did."

"My story is about my father's escape from the Holocaust."

"What's that?" Jim asked.

I explained. "But you mean your grandfather?"

"No," Jennifer replied. "My father. At least that's what he said."

The stories the students told wove a multicultural tapestry. Some were funny, like Nora's running away from home. She was angry, it seemed, because her brothers were having a story read to them and she was supposed to take a nap. Wearing only her diaper, she crawled out the window and walked down a major highway. She was scooped up by a shocked neighbor and returned to her mother, who believed her fast asleep in her crib.

Jennifer's story was, indeed, about her father's escape from the Holocaust. We learned that her father, a fourteen-year-old at the time, worked as a slave laborer in a factory in Eastern Europe, making boots for the Nazi army. He managed to escape through an electrified barbed wire fence one night in the winter of 1944, and made his way to the West. He hid in sewers and haystacks and barns by day. He traveled at night, eating whatever he could steal or whatever the occasional secret host could spare, until he met the advancing allied armies. At fifteen he was enrolled in high school in Boston. At sixteen, he entered Harvard.

Jennifer told her story the night parents came to visit our Family History Museum. Afterwards her mother confided to me that her husband had never told anyone that story until Jennifer asked. Even she had not known it.

"Telling the story has had a healing effect on our family," she said. "Thank you, Mrs. Lipke."

"Thank you," I said. "It was a powerful lesson for us all."

There were other stories. Juan told one about a great-great-great-great- (he didn't know how many) grandfather who saved himself from being eaten by South American jungle cannibals. He happened to have some exploding black powder in his pocket as his captors prepared to roast him. Juan's story was probably apocryphal, but it was welcome nonetheless.

Caroline's family story took us to a cotton field where her ancestor laid her infant son in a ditch to keep him cool. She left his two-year-old sister to watch as she picked cotton. As she neared the end of the field where the children were, she heard a strangled cry. She rushed toward the sound to find that the two-year-old had buried the baby "to keep him cool."

Where before some students had felt scorned or isolated, they now understood each other because they learned about each other's customs and beliefs. They had heard the stories.

A Bridge to School Success

Storytelling does something else, something that may be even more important. It gives a voice to students who find reading and writing to be overwhelming tasks. In inner-city schools where academics are resisted, where the first language is not English, and where other concerns block out the standard curriculum, storytelling may provide the key that unlocks the door to academic achievement. Many of these students come from families where storytelling is still a family tradition. If they come to school and find that the tradition is honored there as well, teachers may find storytelling provides a bridge to school success.

Storytelling and Science? You Betcha! 3

The Challenge

"I'd like you to try to put storytelling and science together," the assistant superintendent for curriculum said to me one spring day the year I was Teacher as Storyteller.

"No problem," I told her. "We already do. When second graders tell stories about animal habits and habitats, they've researched that information, and they're doing storytelling and science."

"No," she said. "Not that. I'm looking for something more profound; something that gets at the essence of science."

"Sure," I said. "I'll think about it."

What was she talking about? How could I do that? I thought and thought. Nothing came to mind.

When you're stuck, it's time to call in an expert. Who is an expert? Someone from out of town! And who is the expert whose advice you can afford? Someone in the family! I telephoned my son, a professor of biochemistry.

"Peter," I said, "we have a problem."

"We, Ma?" he asked.

That was the first of many conversations.

"What do we want to prove?" he asked me.

"That science and storytelling go together," I said.

There was a long silence. Unable to stand it any longer, I added, "I could tell a story."

"Aha!" said Peter. "And I could ask the students what else they wanted to know about the story. Maybe we could use their questions as the basis of a scientific discussion. But what if they don't ask any questions?"

"My students," I said, "are made of questions!"

Experiments

To make a long story short, Peter visited my classroom. We put two fifth grades together, and Peter and I told the class that they were about to be the first class of fifth graders anywhere to be part of an important experiment. That hooked them! Then I told the story of *Bembleman's Bakery* by Melinda Greene. In the story, children in one family make bread that turns out to have a unique quality: each bite tastes of all the wonderful things you ever wanted to eat.

When I finished, Peter asked the students what else they wanted to know about the story. The questions started to flow.

"How did they make the bread?" Jimmy called out.

"What did they put into the bread?"

"What's the recipe?"

"How did the dough cook when so much of it was out of the oven?"

"What made the bread rise?" Marian asked.

"Yeast makes bread rise," said Carolyn.

"What makes yeast work?"

"How can we make the bread and make all that money?"

"If the Bembleman children grew, how could they measure by the size of their hands?"

Peter wrote all their questions on the board. When we had about thirty, Peter stopped and looked at the blackboard.

"Let's see if we can organize these questions," he said.

The students began to come up with categories and divide the questions among them. They argued about which category each question belonged in and agreed that some belonged in more than one. Finally, when each question had been assigned to at least one category, Peter asked them which category was most important. The students debated and then voted.

"OK," he said. "We can only answer one question at a time. You've said 'How the Bread Was Made' is the most important category to investigate. Which question shall we start with?" The most important question, the students decided, had to do with ingredients.

"How are we going to answer the question?" Peter asked.

"Ask an expert!" Joan called.

"Ask the Bemblemans," said Mark.

"Try to make the bread!"

"Experiment!"

"What kind of experiment?"

And so began the hypotheses about how to answer the question by experimentation.

Half an hour later, it was clear that by using the story (and most stories will do) Peter had led the students through the whole scientific method. That is, we had defined a problem we wanted to investigate (how to make the bread), asked questions about the problem, discussed possible answers (hypotheses), designed experiments to test the hypotheses, and decided which hypothesis and which experiment looked most promising.

We hadn't actually done any experiments—that came later—but we had done all the rest. And the story provided the stimulus for the process! Bingo! Scientific method *and* storytelling!

It was a long session, but most of the fifty students remained involved and excited throughout.

Next, Peter and I repaired to the eighth grade and repeated the session. I told the same story and Peter asked what else the students wanted to know about the story.

While the fifth grade had been interested in chemical questions (how the unusual bread was made), the eighth graders, true adolescents, were more interested in the people problems.

"Why did the kids hide under the bed?"

"Why didn't they clean up the mess before their parents came home?"

"How come Sol hid in the woods?"

We switched gears. Again all questions were welcome, but this time the categories dealt with human relations and psychology. They identified categories, singled out the most important question, and designed experiments to answer the questions. Scientific method and storytelling again!

Later, Peter repeated the experiment with his wife's students. Anne taught in a vocational high school in New York City. Her students were inner-city students, mostly black and Hispanic, streetwise, not academically oriented. Their school experience had taught them that they were stupid and they believed that only dumb kids ask questions. That made it harder. I wasn't there, but Anne had her students videotape the session and I watched it later.

Anne told a Native American story, the one about when Creator was making people cookies. Coyote, the mischief maker, was being a nuisance. He distracted Creator and the first batch of cookies burned black. Creator scolded Coyote and started again. Again Coyote talked and interfered, and the next batch of cookies was pale and underdone. Creator lost his temper and sent Coyote packing. He made a third batch and the cookies turned out just right: reddish-brown.

"Oh my gosh," I thought. "She told a racial story. What are the students going to do with that?"

They did quite a lot with it. After several minutes of silence, when Peter thought the whole experiment was a disaster and Anne kept telling him to wait, the questions began. She had indeed told a racial story and the students were intrigued. They asked questions about race, about racial origins, and then, about diseases that were racially tagged: sickle cell anemia, high blood pressure. They asked about AIDS.

These questions were sophisticated and clearly of concern to the students. Peter answered some of them and was able to tell the students where to find the answers to others. Still others, he told them, were questions scientists were currently working in their labs to answer.

Those students not only learned about scientific method. They learned something much more important: they learned that asking questions is valuable, that it leads to knowledge, and that scientists, one of the professions they considered elite and unattainable, worked by asking questions. Their natural curiosity was validated, not squelched. What a lesson!

This method of making scientific method easily understandable and of demystifying science as a subject can be followed by any teacher using almost any story. You don't have to be a scientist, and you don't have to be a professional storyteller.

Try "The Three Little Pigs." Tell the story you remember with enthusiasm and suspense. Throw in some humor if you're comfortable with that. Ask your students what else they want to know about the story. Accept all questions without judging them. I'm willing to bet that before long you'll have a blackboard full of questions on wind velocity, lung capacity, comparative strengths of different building materials, different architectural designs, and eating habits, for starters. You only have to be willing to follow where the students lead, to encourage questioning and exploration. Isn't that what science is?

Two other things are important: wait time, being sure that all the students get a chance to ask questions, not just the "eager beavers," and feeling comfortable saying "I don't know the answer to that question. Let's see if we can find out."

Results

The students learned what scientific method was and how it worked. We learned too—to wait out the questions, to accept *all* questions, to trust the students and the story, and to see links where we had not seen links before. We learned that the "jumping off" places for learning about science can come from unexpected sources, that students of all ages and abilities can ask surprisingly searching questions that may open up new areas to explore and think about. And the assistant superintendent had her "profound" link between storytelling and science!

I explained this way of getting kids to understand scientific method to Fred Stein, then Education Director of the Acton, Massachusetts, Discovery Museums. He was interested in getting kids excited about experiments he had already planned for them. He turned the tables on me, challenging me to create a story that would stimulate questions leading to one or more of those experiments. We walked through the museum.

"Look at this," he said. He balanced a Ping-Pong ball on the air flow from a hand-held hair dryer. He moved a transparent tube through the air above the Ping-Pong ball. As the tube passed several inches above the ball, the ball popped up through the tube and fell to the ground.

"How does that work?" I asked. "Does the hair dryer blow the ball up the tube?"

"No, not really. The difference in air pressure sucks the ball into the tube."

Stories

I went home and thought fiction. The result of that day at the museum was an original story I call "Storm!" about two ordinary kids who go exploring in the desert and get caught in a flash flood in a canyon (see Appendix A).

"Storm!" provides stimulus for questions in multiple areas: air currents, thunder, lightning, rainbows, permeability of soil, waterpower, flash floods, erosion, optics, shadows and color perception, on top of which, there is a clear lesson about keeping a close eye on the weather and wearing clothes that are sensible for the environment.

Another time, Fred talked to me about the qualities of soap bubbles.

"I can make a soap bubble last almost forever," he said. "And I can predict exactly when a soap bubble is going to break!"

"How?"

He encouraged me to experiment.

"Did you know that Magic Markers are different?" Fred is an enthusiastic educator and scientist. I did more experiments. Then I went home and wrote "Bubbles and Paper Towels."

I sent the story off to Fred. "Is it OK?" I asked. "I mean, scientifically?"

"Fine," he said, "but the stick has to be wet."

Easy to fix. I put a puddle at the bottom of the hole. This story is a mystery that the police can't solve but the heroine, a fourth grader, can and does, using what she's learned in science class (see Appendix A).

We tried "Bubbles and Paper Towels" on a combined third- and fourth-grade class. We went through the same process, only this time, when the students asked questions, when they had put forth hypotheses and designed experiments, the experiments were ready to go. Once the questions Fred anticipated had been asked, it was hard for him to wait until all the students had raised their questions, but we did and heard them all.

Now the students were motivated and especially observant because the questions they were answering were ones *they* had asked. They blew soap bubbles—big ones—almost big enough to imprison a compact little brother. They stabbed the bubbles with straws, both wet and dry, and studied the bubbles to see if they could predict when they would break. Later, they did paper chromatography with different Magic Markers and compared results. They learned to repeat experiments to make sure their findings weren't just a "fluke." The story had pointed them toward both sets of experiments.

Writing these stories was not difficult. They involve simple "formula writing" (like romance novels). Figure out what experiment you want to do: What is the problem the experiment is set up to solve? Create a hero or heroine who is about the age of your students (that will help them identify with the protagonist) and put the characters in a situation that will lead to questions the experiment will answer. The story you create and tell will get your students involved. They will become detectives and try to solve the mystery. When students are in-volved in the design and purpose of their work—learning—they are motivated and eager. What teacher could ask for more?

More Ideas

I talked to other teachers and to college professors who train teachers. Alice Naylor, of Appalachian State University, said "Of course stories, storytelling, and science go together. Why, there are books in which the protagonist uses scientific method to solve her problem."

"Such as?" I asked.

"Such as *How to Eat Fried Worms, Maurice's Room, The Beast of M. Racine.*"

I checked those books and some others. She was right. It was a new idea for me.

"I tell stories," Alice said, "to teach my students the importance of using correct scientific names."

I thought about that. Names are an important part of human culture. The importance of names shows up again and again in tradi-tional tales. For many cultures they represent power. Consider "Rumpelstiltskin." It was the power of knowing the little man's name that allowed the queen to keep her baby.

In the creation tales of many cultures it is the *naming* that cre-ates the object:

> In the beginning, Ra rose from the still waters that were Nun. Great was his power . . . It lay in his name and in his naming.
>
> "Shu," he cried and there was the wind. "Tefnut, the spitter!" and it rained. So it was with Nut, the arch of the sky, and Geb, the earth, and all the other things that Ra named and created. (Green 1970)

There are also many Native American stories of this type. Names are important to the study of science. *Carbon* describes the properties of the element; it *is* the element. Telling students stories that emphasize the importance and power of names provides them with a rationale for learning correct scientific terminology.

I began to investigate other ways to tie science and storytelling together. I remembered when the assistant superintendent had first challenged me with this task. I'd thought about the second graders and their animal habits and habitats. The stories they'd told were certainly natural science, and when I went to the library to investigate, I found lots of books for children and adults, both fiction and nonfiction, that dealt with natural science either incidentally or as an essential part of the plot. Stories like these can be read aloud, or parts of them told.

What is the difference between reading aloud and storytelling? There is a world of difference. Reading aloud is important but storytelling is important too. Instead of seeing the printed page, you and your listeners visualize what is happening in the story. Together, you are transported to the woods where the vixen is taking care of her kits or the rabbit is teaching her little ones to hide and freeze when danger is near. Your students smell the early morning dew on the grass and feel the wetness between their bare toes. They see the cobwebs jeweled with dew, the colors muted by early morning mist. What a gift to give them! And they can tell stories too. The results are astonishing. The information they hear and tell about becomes part of them. They will remember it long after they have forgotten information learned from textbooks. Children have an enormous and detailed memory of stories they have heard and told.

Stories Have Many Lessons

I thought some more. I remembered the excitement I had felt when, as a teenager, I read Paul De Kruif's *Microbe Hunters*. I told my students the story of Paul Ehrlich's "Magic Bullet." Imagine doing six hundred and five unsuccessful experiments and not being discouraged. Imagine the excitement of finding that number six hundred and six not only worked, but became the "cure" for syphilis, the nineteenth-century equivalent of AIDS. Think of the lessons there! Persistence in the face of failure. Learning from our mistakes. I also told my students the story of Louis Pasteur's discovery of a cure for rabies, a wonderful tale with all the suspense and pathos of a soap opera!

The stories of the lives of scientists and of their discoveries make excellent storytelling material.

Older students can explore and discuss ethical problems that arise in real scientific situations. Tell these stories: Who did discover the double helix? Watson and Crick, who got the Nobel Prize for it, or an almost forgotten woman in a London laboratory? What happened to a distinguished Nobel laureate when a collaborator published a paper with his name on it that turned out to be based on doctored results? This one is still a mystery. Mysteries and crimes! Tell the stories as courtroom dramas and let students be the jury!

Stories Promote Research

In workshops I have given since I left the classroom, I have asked participants to brainstorm a list of natural phenomena: rainbows, floods, thunder and lightning, rain, mountains, rivers, things rusting, fruit ripening, the metamorphosis of insects—

"And tadpoles!" a participant called.

"Good list. Now, choose one of the phenomena on our list and make up a myth about how that happened, what caused it. Be as imaginative as you like. You have three minutes to tell your myth to a partner."

The participants got to work creating myths and sharing them. Some were original, and some were classic myths they remembered.

If I were working with a class, I would have the students tell or write down their myths. When they were finished we would share them and then I would group students by topic and set them to work to research, experiment, and try to come up with scientific explanations.

Ecology

Ecology is another area of science that lends itself well to storytelling. There is a lot of important information for students (and adults) to learn about the science of ecology. Wonderful stories can make the point. (Some of these can be found in a book by Ed Brody and his storytelling colleagues called *Spinning Tales, Weaving Hope.*) One of my favorites is a story that has been making its way around the storytelling community for some time. The idea comes from "The Glass Cupboard" by Terry Jones (in *Fairy Tales* by the same author). "The Crystal Cabinet" is an allegory about how we must replenish the earth if we are to keep benefiting from its gifts. It's a story that might have a medieval setting and it's a story with good guys and bad guys (see Appendix A).

Tell this story and others like it to your students. Discuss their meaning. Then ask them to do some research and create their own ecology stories.

A Key to Science Mysteries

Part of the trouble with science in the elementary schools is the result of fear. Very few elementary teachers majored in science or have had jobs in science labs. Even in middle school, a teacher may sometimes be assigned to teach science whose science education may consist of one undergraduate course or a science methods course, a situation that does not make for comfortable teaching. Like everyone else, teachers tend to be afraid of what they do not know or have been told is "too difficult." When teachers are afraid, they avoid.

Science is exciting. It is the stuff of curiosity and we were all born with large doses of curiosity! It is the stuff of imagination and wondering. Scientists don't know all the answers. They are curious folk looking for answers. This is the message teachers and students need to hear. And where do you find the questions to ask? In the world around us, including the world of story and imagination.

Aren't myths how science got started? People were curious about such things as rainbows, floods, thunder and lightning, rain, mountains, rivers, things rusting, fruit ripening, the metamorphosis of insects and tadpoles. Because they didn't have the technology to answer the questions scientifically, they created myths to explain them. We can use myths and stories to lead students to understand and enjoy science. You might say that the wheel has come full circle.

Storytelling and Math Intersect $\quad$ 4

Exploring the Problem

I had heard of using storytelling to teach math. I read a paper about it. I attended a workshop. It was logical. If it worked for science and social studies, why not math? Why not, indeed? Goodness knows there are plenty of stories, songs, and games that have math in them. The first ones I thought of were "One, two buckle my shoe; Three, four, close the door . . ." and "Ten Little Indians."

Of course there are lots of counting rhymes and stories, but how could they apply to teaching math outside of the obvious applications of counting from one to ten?

Other stories that were familiar to me as a storyteller had obvious math applications. There was the classic story of the invention of chess, the Greek myth about Anteus who redoubled his strength each time he touched the earth, fairy tale heroes with seven league boots. I thought of a traditional Japanese tale about a magic paddle that makes more rice (see Appendix A).

I went to a workshop given by Deb Socia, a teacher from southeastern Massachusetts. She told an original story about a hero she had invented, "Super Teddy," who helped her children learn how to group numbers for counting. She gave him a theme song and invited her students to invent new counting adventures for him. I learned about the work of Virginia Usnick, David Whitin, and Sandra Wilde, who work with math and children's literature. But I wanted something more, something like the discovery Peter and I had made about how to find "scientific method" in any story. Could I do that with math? The assistant superintendent's challenge stuck with me. Was there a way to get at the essence of math through storytelling?

I pursued the question further. My friend Katie Hereld sent me a paper she had written for an education course. I followed the trail and met by phone with Rita Hughes, a storyteller and retired kindergarten teacher from Cheshire, Connecticut. What a treasure trove of creative ideas Rita turned out to be.

"All you really have to do," she said, "is think mathematically. Then any story has math possibilities and implications."

What Is Math?

What is math anyway? I looked it up in the dictionary: "The group of sciences (including arithmetic, geometry, algebra, calculus, etc.) dealing with quantities, magnitudes and forms, and their relationships, attributes, etc. by use of numbers and symbols."

Then I asked kids—from kindergarten through seventh grade—because they are the ones we work with, and we need to understand what they know.

I started researching math and storytelling. I spoke to colleagues. I read. I borrowed classrooms and students. I worked with different grade levels and school settings. I began each lesson by asking the students, "What is math?" They had a variety of definitions:

"Math is the relationships of numbers and values."

"Different ways of using numbers."

"Addition."

"Subtraction."

But I'm getting ahead of myself. My first venture into the practical world of research with math and storytelling came when I stepped into a colleague's fourth-grade classroom. I was introduced as a storyteller who was trying an experiment.

"What is math?" I asked.

As the children called out their definitions, I wrote the list on the board:

"Adding!"

"Subtraction."

"Times."

"Division."

"Fractions." (There was a groan somewhere in the room.)

"Percent."

"Numbers and their relationships." (That was pretty close to Webster's definition.)

"Operations."

When the board was full and they had run out of definitions, I said, "Let me tell you a story."

Once upon a time there was a king who had done all the kingly things and done them very well. He ruled his kingdom wisely. He had fought and won the wars with overweening former neighbors, killed off the monsters and dragons; he was a patron of the arts, he danced well, and told stories well; he was a fine husband and father. He knew how to work and how to play but at last, he was bored. There was nothing new in the world for him to do.

He turned to his Grand Vizier (chief courtier in some versions) and asked him to invent a game that would always be interesting and challenging. The Grand Vizier bowed and asked for some time to think. The king graciously granted his wish.

Three days later, the Grand Vizier returned to the court with a new game: chess.

The king played the game with the Grand Vizier. He played it with the queen, with his grandchildren, with everyone. Sometimes he won and sometimes he lost, for he was a king who was not afraid to lose. The game was always different, always interesting. It always presented new challenges and new strategies to work out.

The king was delighted. He summoned the Grand Vizier.

"This is truly a wonderful game," he said. "It does all I asked. Please, take half my kingdom and my daughter's hand in marriage as your reward."

"Oh, Your Majesty is much too generous," the Grand Vizier replied. "I could not take half your kingdom, and I do not think my wife would be happy were I to marry your beautiful and wise daughter."

"Of course," replied the king. "Forgive me. I had momentarily forgotten Mrs. Vizier. Please name your own reward."

The Grand Vizier thought for a few minutes and then he bowed to the king. "All I want, Your Majesty, is a grain of rice."

"What?" cried the astonished king.

"Just one grain of rice," the Grand Vizier continued, "on the first square of the chessboard, two grains of rice on the second square, four grains of rice on the third square, eight on the fourth, and just double the amount on each of the sixty-four squares of the chessboard."

"Surely, you are too modest in your request," His Majesty remonstrated. But the Grand Vizier insisted that that was all he wanted. So the king ordered that his loyal Grand Vizier be rewarded as he had asked.

That is where I stopped. The end of the story is that it was not long before the royal granaries were emptied and all the rice in the kingdom, the kingdom itself, and several kingdoms beyond, belonged to the clever and ambitious Grand Vizier.

"What questions do you have about the story?" I asked the students.

"How much rice was it?" was the first question—and the only one the students seemed to care about.

I pulled out a five-pound bag of rice, my photocopies of a chess board, and some plastic containers. Each group of children got chessboards and shared a container of rice.

In this first class the question of calculators came up almost at once.

"Calculators are fine," I told them. "Any way you can figure out the answer is OK."

"Paper and pencil?"

"Sure."

"We've got the answer!" Jenny called out.

"What is it?" I asked.

"Four thousand ninety-six!"

"I don't think that's it."

"Yes, it is. We multiplied sixty-four times sixty-four."

"No," said David. "It's bigger than that!"

"Do we have to use the chessboards and rice?"

"No."

"I got an answer but there's a little *E* on my calculator."

"That means there's an error," someone said.

They discovered that the calculators became useless by the twenty-eighth square.

"How much rice was it?"

"Somewhere in the quintillions," I said.

"But," David said, "even if you know how much rice there is on the sixty-fourth square, that's not the answer."

I smiled. David was thinking. "What do you mean?"

"You still have to add up all the rice on each square!"

"You're right!" I told him.

Their time, and mine, had run out. Only when I got home did I realize that I had forgotten to ask them two essential questions:

Do you want to change or add to your definition of math?

What did you learn?

I didn't make that mistake again!

I tried the same story with another fourth grade. These students took a long time to think of paper and pencil, and even longer to think of calculators. I prowled around the room. I dropped hints. They continued laboriously counting out grains of rice.

"I keep messing up," Sue said.

"It's hard," John agreed. "These grains of rice are too small."

Eventually they came to the same conclusions as the first class.

When I asked them if they wanted to change their definition of math, they didn't think they did. When I asked them what they had learned, they said they were surprised that a little number could become so big so quickly. They also said that they had found out that math could be fun!

I knew there were many extensions and applications in the story. Deb Socia had told the story in kindergarten and first grade and gotten those students to try estimation. She had used it to teach small and large numbers. I had thought of other extensions for the problem and hadn't yet had a chance to try any of them. For example, how much land would it take to grow that much rice? How many farmers? How long? Where would you put it all? How many grains of rice can you fit on a chessboard square? How about different kinds of rice? How do you account for different sizes of rice grains if you are trying to figure volume or weight? Clearly, there was no limit to the questions about the rice, and I hadn't even begun to think about other kinds of math questions that might arise from different aspects of the story, like linear growth versus exponential growth.

"Maybe," I said to myself, "I should try this with older students." I called my friend Sheila, who teaches advanced seventh-grade math.

"May I come and tell a story to your math class?"

"Sure. What day?"

I went to her school and went through my now familiar routine with her students. Their math definitions were a little more sophisticated than those of the fourth graders. They included formulas, variables, sets, patterns, and "different ways of using numbers."

I told the same story. The students quickly got to work trying to find the answer to the problem: How much rice was it? I roamed the room. I saw one young man standing with his back to the rest of the class, his nose almost on the wall. What was he doing? I moved closer. He had discovered a wall chart that showed the powers of two. He was carefully counting the lines to sixty-four! Aha! There are many ways to solve a problem!

I asked the students if they could figure out a formula to come up with the answer. I asked them if they could figure the weight and volume of such an amount of rice. Sheila rummaged in her files and came up with an article by Carl Sagan from a 1989 *Parade* magazine. Dr. Sagan told the story with wheat instead of rice. (It's a traditional tale with many versions.) He figured that 18.8 quintillion grains of wheat would weigh about 75 billion metric tons, about the weight of the earth! He didn't figure the volume.

I had another related problem for them: "The printed chessboards that you have are smaller than the standard chessboard because a standard chessboard won't copy onto a standard piece of paper. The printed chessboards are a 64 percent reduction of a regular chessboard. How much rice could you fit on a square of a standard chessboard?"

I asked them to jot down any further extensions they could think of for the problem.

One girl defined the size of each piece of rice and wanted to know how many standard chessboards the total amount of rice would fill. Another student wanted to work out a formula to find the answer. Still another student wanted to solve the problem on a spreadsheet.

"Graph the answer."

"Find the patterns."

I asked if they wanted to change their original definition of math. Most of them did.

"Math," one boy wrote, "is everything that has to do with numbers and values and the way to describe them: theories, formulas, etc. It follows one set of rules."

There were a good many additions: logic, tessellations, powers, math thinking. I asked them what they had learned from the lesson.

"I learned it's impossible to count to a trillion."

"I learned that there is always more than one way to solve a problem."

"I think now of math having more to do with everyday things. Before I thought math was just the pointless problems you would only have to know if you were a teacher or an architect."

"I learned that if you work with a group you can use each other's ideas and everyone can help solve the problem."

Without question, this story, with its obvious math applications, worked. Furthermore, the students were able to use the story as a jumping-off place for other math applications and ideas. They could create and discover their own problems and meanings.

Math Is Universal

I wanted to experiment further and see if I could find a way to use any story to teach math, as Rita Hughes had suggested. Was any story a math story? Could storytelling be used to get at the essence of math, just as Peter and I had discovered any story could be used to get at the essence of science? I tried some of her ideas.

A first grade helped me tell the story of "Goldilocks and the Three Bears." When we had finished I asked them if there was any math in the story. The hands shot up!

"How big were each of the bears?"

"How big were each of the chairs?"

"Beds?"

"Bowls of porridge?"

"How sweet was the porridge?" (Chemistry?)

"How much porridge was in each bowl?"

"How much was left in each bowl after Goldilocks ate?"

"How far did the bears walk? How far did Goldilocks walk?"

"How many feet were there in the story—bears' feet, Goldilocks' feet?"

"Chairs' feet, table's feet, beds' feet!"

"How high was the window Goldilocks jumped from?"

They had more. We put their questions in categories: measurement, comparative size, temperature, counting, addition, multiplication.

When I had to cut them short because time was running out, they were preparing to ask each other the problems and work out the answers.

"What did you learn about math and storytelling?" I asked.

"That math can be lots of fun!"

"That math is everywhere in the world if you just think math!"

Give that student a gold star and send her to the top of the class!

There it was. Math is everywhere in the world if you just think math. Storytelling does make math more fun, and it also makes the concepts easier to understand and remember. And if the students set up the problems, they have a vested interest in solving them.

I thought mathematically about "Rumpelstiltskin." How much gold did the miller's daughter have to spin? Suppose the room in which the king imprisoned her was twelve-feet square with an eight-foot ceiling. How much gold thread would a room like that hold? Were the straw and thread in a one-to-one ratio? Another kind of math problem! Give your students extra practice by varying the ratio!

How hard did Rumpelstiltskin stamp when he stamped himself into the earth? What was the force behind his foot stamping?

How far had the messengers traveled when they were trying to learn Rumpelstiltskin's name? How about mapping their travels? How about time and distance problems?

Plenty of math questions. And it worked with "Sleeping Beauty," "Little Red Riding Hood," any story. Try thinking math yourself. What applications can you find?

I tried this method with middle school students and I told a much more sophisticated story—one I usually tell to adult audiences. The story is a traditional one about selkies, seal people, called "Angus Raudh, the Seal Killer." Below is a sample of the problems they created after hearing the story:

> The man dropped 400 feet off the cliff into the water averaging 5 feet per second. How many seconds did it take to reach the surface of the water? Write your answer as a fraction.

> If the seal killer killed three seals in two hours, how many days and hours would it take him to kill 100 seals if he worked nine hours a day?

> If the wind was blowing thirty miles per hour and the horse was going faster than the wind, and yet they were going slower than the wind in front of them, how fast were they going?

The more sophisticated the story and the more advanced the students, the more complex the problems they find in the story. Clearly, any story will serve as a stimulus to create math problems.

Perhaps that was the key I sought. Not only were there math applications in any story, but there were math applications beyond the obvious ones, even in a math-specific story. Math applications can be specific but they need not be exclusive. Think math!

Math-Specific Stories
Math to Count
Let's go back to the beginning of this chapter.

> *"One, two, buckle my shoe;*
> *Three, four, close the door . . ."*

What math does a child learn from this rhyme? To count, of course, and to count by twos. How about "Ten Little Indians"? The obvious applications are counting up and counting down, and counting by twos, but also one-to-one ratio, addition, subtraction, multiplication, division, fractions, and percentages.

Many folktales are counting stories. One of my favorites comes from the Middle East. I found a version in Turkey (see Appendix A). Nasradin has trouble counting the donkeys he's taking to the mill because he always forgets to count the one he's riding. Only when he gets off are there the right number of donkeys.

I tried this story with a kindergarten class. The children knew how to count, but like Nasradin, they often forgot to count themselves. They acted out the story and giggled over Nasradin's dilemma. Their teacher reported that after that, whenever anyone missed in counting because they forgot to count themselves, the other students called out "Nasradin!" It became a code word!

Counting, of course, is the obvious math application in this story, but its applications can be expanded to include fractions, percentages, measurement (of loads), mapping, time-distance-rate-of-travel problems—and your students may think of others!

Math to Measure and Estimate
In a second-grade class, after asking the students for their definitions of math, I told a traditional Japanese story about a little old woman and her rice cakes and how she learned from monsters that with a magic paddle, one grain of rice could make many rice cakes. When I finished telling the story, I asked what math questions they had about it.

> "How did the rice get bigger?"
> "How big was the monster?"
> "How fast did she run?"

"How could she run twice as fast when she was already running her fastest?"
"How far did she run?"
"How much water was in the river?"
"How big is 256 grains of rice?"
"How could you find out?" I asked them.
"We could count."

Out came the bag of rice. I gave each group a small container of rice. Each student got a piece of colored construction paper for the grains of rice (that made it easier for them to see the individual grains, and it made it easier to keep the rice on the desks). They started counting. One group figured out that if they made groups of ten they could keep track of the counting more easily. Other groups tried the same system.

"They're copying us," the first group complained.

"You found a good method and they see it's a better way to count. They want to copy you because your way works."

"Oh." Somewhat mollified they continued to count.

After a while, I pulled out plastic envelopes of 256 precounted grains of rice. Even though by then, many of the children had figured out ways to group the numbers and count more easily, no one had reached the magic number of 256. The amount of rice in the plastic envelopes looked awfully small.

"Are you sure this is a whole 256 grains of rice?" asked Jennie, who had struggled and finally gotten to a hundred.

"Does it look like it's double what you've counted and some more?"

"I guess so." She clearly wasn't sure at all. "Is that enough to fill the pot?" she asked.

"What do you think?"

I pulled out another plastic container and gave each group a small mound of cooked rice.

"This isn't the same," Eddie complained.

"Is this rice?"

"It's different."

"Different than what?" I asked.

"Different than this." Eddie pointed to his raw rice.

"Yes," I explained. "This rice is cooked. What do you notice?"

"It's bigger!"

"Why?" I asked.

They looked blank.

"How do you cook rice?" I asked. My question was greeted with more blank looks and silence.

Finally Sally ventured, "In the microwave?"

"Sometimes," I said. "But always in liquid. The rice absorbs some of the liquid. Do you think 256 grains of cooked rice would fill the pot?"

They didn't think so and they were right, of course. It was just about a good rounded tablespoon of rice. But, they had figured out that counting by groups was easier when they were dealing with big numbers, and they had done some estimation. They had also dealt with volume—of both raw rice and cooked rice.

If we had considered Caroline's question ("How big was the monster?"), we would have worked with comparative sizes. If we had pursued the amount of water in the river, we would have worked with volume, numbers of monsters, and their mouth capacities. There were questions that dealt with speed, energy, and distance.

Even though I thought of that story as specific to doubling, measuring, and estimation, the students found many more applications! There were a lot of questions, a lot of working with manipulative materials, and a lot of interest in learning how to work out the answers.

When I asked my two standard end-of-lesson questions, they weren't sure about how to change their definitions of math, but someone mentioned grouping numbers for the first time. As for what they had learned, they told me they enjoyed the story, they learned that math could be fun, and that cooked rice was sticky and messy.

Their teacher asked me, "Is this math or science?"

I was startled by her question. The answer came quickly. What did it matter? We know that math and science intersect all the time. What mattered was that the students were curious. They were asking questions that they wanted to answer. Isn't that what education is all about? Right back to Socrates sitting on his log?

Venn Diagrams Too!

There are more ways that math and storytelling intersect. You might, for example, ask a class what they remember about the story of Cinderella. They probably know at least the Disney version. They can brainstorm while you write down the points they bring up on the board.

Give your students strips of paper and ask them to write one important element of the story on each strip. Then tell them another version of Cinderella. There are more than five hundred. You could tell them the classic version which is pretty gory (the stepsisters cut off their toes or heel to try to fit their feet into the glass slipper). Or tell them the Zulu version called "Nomi and the Magic Fish," or the Chinese version called "Yeh Shen" (Sierra 1992).

Again, have them write each important element of the story on a strip of paper and then move the strips around so that the elements that are the same are together in the middle. If they put circles of wool, or even draw circles, around the three groups of slips, you'll have a Venn diagram:

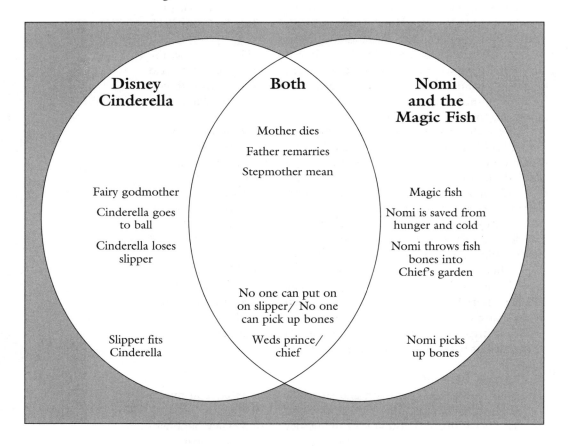

Your students will probably want to say that the fairy godmother and the magic fish are common elements, and they will surely find other commonalities. That's just fine. As they work, you can write your own lists on a transparency and draw circles around the elements in each story. When you switch on the overhead you will have modeled your Venn diagram. The advantage of strips of paper is that the students can move them around so the common elements will end up together. This idea comes from work done by Virginia Usnick (see References).

Extend your students' math thinking. Put them in groups and ask them to tell each other any other traditional stories they know, to find other versions, and then to create their own Venn diagrams. They will discover their own intersections of storytelling and math.

Other Kinds of Stories

Go back to mythology. Do you remember Antaeus? He was the son of Gaea, the earth. Each time he touched the earth he redoubled his strength. Heracles had to fight him. He finally beat Antaeus when he picked him up and strangled him in the air. It is an exciting story. You can tell it as a sports announcer reporting a wrestling match. Try the hold-by-hold, fall-by-fall approach. Your middle-grade students will be caught up in the excitement of the match. They will think up half a dozen problems to solve related to that myth; problems dealing with force, doubling, measurement, timing, and fractions—and they'll probably find other math applications. If you are also studying Greek mythology you will have doubled your purpose by telling the myth.

Think back to all the stories you know or heard when you were little. You can even tell stories from appropriate movies and television shows. There are resources upon resources. You only need to think math!

Original Stories

As in science, you can make up your own math-related stories to tell. You can tailor them to the kind of math you want your students to investigate. For example, the story of Rosie and David is another mystery. Kids love mysteries and they love it when the hero and heroine help solve the mystery. Rosie and David go fishing and catch a large amount of money—probably forty or fifty thousand dollars—they don't have time to count it so they estimate. What happens next is what they do with the unexpected windfall and how they help pinpoint the criminal! (See Appendix A.)

Here's a mystery to solve. You can use the story to teach specific math lessons in estimation (have your students cut out paper and try the thumb method). The story is also good for teaching counting, grouping of numbers, money, equality, measurement, multiplication, comparative weights (of the garbage bags with and without the water), volume (of water in the bags), mapping, or time in the tide rise and fall. Or turn your students loose and let them find (and solve) the math problems they discover. You can use the story for science, too: tides, fog, currents, kinds of soil, what grew or got caught on the outside garbage bag are just starters.

As in the last chapter, with the science and ecology stories, you can use this story as a prototype and create your own—or challenge your students to create and tell their own stories. I like the idea of a mystery in math: there's always at least one problem to solve.

Biography and History

You can also tell stories of the lives of mathematicians and the history of mathematics. I suppose the oldest math story I know is the story of Archimedes in his bath:

> King Hiero II commanded that Archimedes find out whether his crown was made of solid gold or of gold and silver alloy. Of course, Archimedes couldn't melt the crown down or damage it in any way. It was a difficult problem and he thought and thought about it. He thought about it as he ate. He thought about it as he slept, as he walked to market, as he sat in his library.
>
> He got into his bath one day, enjoying the warm water and cogitating about his problem. Suddenly he realized that the bath was overflowing. Hm. He must have gained more weight. Too much of his wife's good cooking. More water displacement, that's what it was. Suddenly, he realized that gold and silver had different water displacements! He could weigh the crown, then weigh an equal amount of pure gold, and he would know if the crown was pure gold.
>
> He was so excited at finding the solution to his problem that he jumped out of his bath and ran out into the street shouting "Eureka!" (I have found it!). He forgot, in his excitement, to put on his clothes!

Here's a historic instance of math discovery! It's also a fine example of how exciting discoveries can be! Have your students create their own water displacement problems and let the story help you teach the math skills they need to know in order to do the problems.

I remember, years ago, visiting the University of Chicago and "discovering" Ancient Sumer. What I saw in a glass case was a series of small clay shapes: cubes, spheres, pyramids, bricks. The caption told me that each of these shapes represented a certain amount of a particular cargo that was shipped up or down the river: so many bushels of wheat, so many sheep, and so on. The clay shapes were put in a clay envelope and sealed with the impression of the sender's own seal. When the captain of the ship delivered his cargo, it was easy for the man receiving the cargo to break open the clay envelope and check the contents of the shipment against the number and kind of clay shapes enclosed in the envelope. These were the first bills of lading, the first "written" accounting!

I found this information exciting. Think of the stories you could tell based on that bit of math history: tales of river boat captains enriching themselves at the expense of the men who hired them to transport goods, stealing part of their cargo and caught red-handed by the sealed clay envelope that contained those first bills of lading! Tell your students the story and have them create their own systems of numeration and accounting.

Math and Literature

A great deal of children's literature can have math applications, but I will mention only a few books. The one I know best is Norton Juster's classic, *The Phantom Tollbooth*, a thoroughly delightful book to read, to read aloud, and to tell stories from. Every child should meet the Mathemagician and King Azzazz.

There's Edward Eager's book *Half Magic*. In this story children find a coin that gives them half of whatever they wish. As a result, they find themselves in really strange circumstances. Tell your students a bit of the story. Perhaps you have already read the whole book to the class and they are familiar with it. In any case, *telling* the story, rather than reading it aloud, creates a different atmosphere in your classroom. Your students may well know by now that when you tell a story, there is a kind of license for them to take off and be creative. Ask them to figure out how much the children need to wish for in order to make sure their whole wish comes true. Change the fraction. Have the coin give them a third of their wish, or three quarters of their wish. It will give them real motivation for all that division of fractions! Invite your students to create their own dilemmas for the characters in *Half Magic*! They can tell their own versions of the story.

There's a delightful book called *The King's Commissioners* by

Aileen Friedman about how to count to forty-seven in a number of different ways. And there are numerous other books. Moreover, there are a number of people, including Virginia Usnick, David J. Whitin, and Sandra Wilde, who have compiled extensive bibliographies of "math literature." I have listed a few books in Appendix B, mostly as resources of stories or parts of stories, you can tell to get your students hooked on math learning.

It is important for students to know that literature has math applications. Storytelling is different. You and your students can create your own math community of storytelling using your own ideas and imaginations to discover a world of math everywhere. You need not be limited to what you find in the literature. Create stories that fulfill your lesson purposes and challenge your students to do the same. Tell the stories to make math fun and math concepts more understandable.

What advantages do math and storytelling have over math and reading stories aloud? As I mentioned in Chapter 1, when you tell stories, there is no barrier between the storyteller and the audience. A community of sharing is created, with math as well as with any other subject. There is another factor: storytelling is less formal. If you read a book, you visualize the scenes and characters, but you are bound by the author's creativity. How about the teacher's and the students' creativity? Storytelling can free up imaginations and allow, even encourage, original stories and ideas. That's powerful stuff.

A Problem and a Solution

Most elementary teachers, I believe, teach math comfortably and well. Yet there are some who had unhappy experiences with math as students and who are still uncomfortable with it.

I didn't enjoy my elementary math education. Math was hard and most of it was not fun. The answers were either right or wrong, mostly wrong. There didn't seem to be any logic or reason behind the operations. Kids who were lucky got it right. I was mostly unlucky! My breakthrough came when I took a course in Modern Elementary Math one summer before I started my teacher training. Oh, there was a rationale! That was how and why it worked! What a discovery!

When I taught math, I made my lessons as clear as I could. I tried to be sure my students understood the *why* behind the operations. I was comfortable with math, but not inspired. I made it my business to observe outstanding math teachers and learned to include things like mental math and math challenge games in my lessons.

When I started working with storytelling and math, I found that I was enjoying the teaching a lot, and so were the students. Instead of struggling through the assigned work without too many mistakes, the students became excited, involved and eager to try new things. I found myself interested in learning more about math. I found that math was interesting for itself!

When I thought about organizing this chapter according to math disciplines, I had a problem: if I did that, I would limit teachers (and by limiting teachers I'd limit students) to a more rigid, less imaginative use of stories and storytelling in their approach to math. I truly did not want to do that. Teachers can choose stories to tell that deal primarily with counting, as in the story of "Nasradin and the Donkeys," or the powers of numbers, as in the chess story. Or they can say to their classes, "I challenge you to find division problems (or fractions or geometry) in this story." If math is everywhere—and it is—and you look at stories that way it seems counterproductive to limit any story to a particular math discipline. You only need to wait for the students, encourage their ideas, and let them explore and find their own math! Tell stories and break out of the constraints of your math text. Invite your students to find fun in understanding math everywhere.

I was talking with a math professor recently. He told me about a child he knew who was "numerate," a child who understood the language and thought processes of math. How wonderful if we could all be numerate like that first grader, "thinking math!"

Part II

Teaching Storytelling

Guide to Part II

A Teaching Unit

This unit is designed to help teachers teach their students to become storytellers. However, the steps for learning to be a storyteller are universal, so teachers can follow selected directions and improve their storytelling skills as well.

The unit is also designed to teach storytelling as a way to learn. As a method for teaching science and math, storytelling can be much less formal. Polished performance is not the goal.

Storytelling encourages and supports a wide range of language skills:

- Listening
- Response
- Speaking
- Pronunciation (enunciation, correct usage, projection)
- Vocabulary enrichment
- Writing skills (plot, characterization, setting, dialogue, summarizing, imagery)
- Imagination
- Performing for large and small audiences
- Evaluation of self and others

Providing a Safe Environment

Everyone enjoys hearing and telling stories. Through storytelling students grow in skill, imagination, and positive self-image. It's fun—but it's also risky. When one student, all alone, is responsible for commanding the attention of an audience, the teacher must provide a safe and supportive environment.

How can the teacher accomplish this? Summarized below (and spelled out in the following pages) are ways to ensure an environment in which students can take risks. It is a nonthreatening, step-by-step process that includes everybody.

Recommended Steps in Teaching the Unit
Listening to a Story
A good way to begin the storytelling unit is by telling a story. If you feel uncomfortable doing this, you can turn to the many storytelling audio and videotapes available commercially (see Appendix B). Remember, though, that the best teaching is modeling. Even if you are not as polished as a professional storyteller, you make an excellent role model for your students. They will welcome your joining them in learning to tell stories.

Choosing the Story
As teacher, you decide what the focus of the storytelling will be. Depending on what you want to accomplish, the sources may be familiar folktales, or a teacher-created story that illustrates a science or math problem or principle, or something else. Next, each student chooses a story to tell. It is important that each student make a choice, since choice assures motivation and ownership. If students choose stories from their reading, advise them to choose one they really like, because they are going to spend a long time with it. Stories they remember from when they were little and their own creations are also good sources. Books *without illustrations* are best because then children make their own images.

If the storytelling is part of a family history unit, then interviews and attic searches are in order. Interviewing techniques, sample questions, and home resources other than people, are spelled out later (see pp. 80–81). There is also a sample letter to parents.

Once students have chosen their stories, have them sit in a circle and tell everyone *about* their choice. This is different from telling the story. It is a brief summary. This exercise also builds confidence by giving each student an opportunity to share the story's general outline and providing each student with a chance to speak informally to the whole group.

Creating a Story
From time to time you may want a story that is specific to a particular lesson. You can't find one in your resources and don't have time to do a thorough search. Don't panic. Make up your own story. It's easy. I have found the following steps useful:

1. Be sure you know the *purpose* of this story.

2. Create a *hero or heroine* (or a combination) who is about the same age as your students. Make your characters believable, neither "too good" nor "too evil." The closer they are to people you and your students know, the more credible they will be. You know your students and their backgrounds. Stick to the familiar. Beware of caricaturing any particular person: the laughter of recognition may come at someone's expense.

   You may wish to use the same characters in each story, in which case, your students will get to know them and feel very much at home with them. Or you may choose to make your stories individual creations.

3. The *setting*—and how important it is to your story—depends on your purpose. Don't load it with unneccessary details but be sure *you* can visualize it. You should be able to see, smell, hear, taste, and touch it—see the colors, the light, and the shadows. The better you visualize it, the more your students will feel that they are "on the scene."

4. The *plot* of your story is basically the problem that must be solved. Keep it simple and make sure it serves your purpose. It should include some risk, some excitement, a touch of danger, and, of course, a solution.

5. If you want your story to lead to a specific *experiment* or mathematical *problem* or operation, focus the story so that the particular experiment or problem is the most obvious part.

   Make it easy for yourself. Take notes, but don't spend time and energy drafting and polishing. Remember, this is a story *for telling*. It is different from a story for reading. Be sure that your beginning has a good hook and that your ending is satisfying. Use words and phrases that describe the images you see, the emotions you feel. *Don't memorize*. Revision is a natural part of each telling.

   To recap: Know the beginning and end, the characters, the sequence (what happens, in what order), and any particularly good imagery.

Tell your story.

If you are uncomfortable trying it out for the first time with your class, find a rehearsal partner and ask for feedback that is useful and nonthreatening. (More about rehearsal partners and feedback later.) Get into the story and let it tell itself. Remember, it will grow and change with each telling. Let it stay loose and fluid.

Resources

A class trip to the library early in the storytelling unit is invaluable. If a student chooses a long story, help him select which part of it to tell (a five-minute maximum is best). You and the librarian can guide students to appropriate books.

If a student chooses a literary tale from a published collection, crediting the author is an important obligation. The storyteller can say, "This story comes from a book called *Stories* by Mary Johnson." If students present their stories outside the school setting, on local cable television, for example, it is necessary to write the publisher for permission to tell the story. Although the book may be displayed as the storyteller credits the source, the story should be told, not read.

Games

Games are a good way to help students feel at home with storytelling without being self-conscious. Play games before students start the unit and at appropriate times during the process. (Descriptions of storytelling games begin on p. 82. Others will be found in the collections of books about storytelling listed in Appendix B.) One game per session is usually sufficient to get students loosened up. In addition to storytelling games there are also audience participation stories. *Joining In*, compiled by Teresa Miller with assistance from Anne Pellowski, and edited by Norma Livo, has a fine collection of such stories and pointers on how to get an audience participating.

Getting Students Started

Each student should receive copies of student guide sheets as needed. Go over the steps carefully. You may wish to fill out and share sheets for your own story as a model.

Learning the Story

The most difficult part of teaching students to tell stories is convincing them not to memorize it. The object is to get them to "know" the story without memorizing it. There are a number of ways to do this. Here are some ideas. All these exercises, which are explained in detail later in the unit, bring the teller deeper into the story. Choose the way(s) that fit your teaching style and your students' learning styles.

1. Have students use their imaginations to draw pictures and then "tell" the pictures. Indicate colors, sounds, smells, tastes, tactile features.

2. Work with charts (see pp. 91–93). Storytelling Chart I asks students to divide the story into parts, fill in characters, action, mood, and imagery. Storytelling charts II and III help students learn more about their characters and settings.

3. Use teacher-guided imagery (see p. 70) to help students place themselves "in their scene."

4. Make a web of the story (see p. 94).

5. Have students audiotape the story and listen to the tape.

6. Have students learn the sequence of the story and tell it a number of times to themselves and/or a rehearsal partner.

Rehearsing/Conferring

As they work, students tell their stories to a rehearsal partner, a small group, and finally the whole class. Together, the class and the teacher set up a structure similar to the writing process: students confer with each other as they work on stories for performance.

The teller tells her conference partner what kind of feedback she wants: "Is the story clear?" "Do I speak distinctly?" "Can you 'see' the settings?" "Are the characters believable?" "Can you tell who is speaking?"

Requests for responses should be specific: "Is there any place where you get confused as you listen?"

"It was all clear, except I couldn't tell just what happened when the dragon knocked the horse over."

Please remind students that one response request at a time is enough. This focuses the listener and allows the teller to concentrate on the area where he wants feedback.

Remind students that the story "belongs" to the teller. Once the teller decides to tell a story, it is his. There are no "wrong" ways to tell a story, only different versions. The listener responds to the storyteller by addressing the specific conference request and by telling the teller, specifically, what worked in this telling. The purpose of the conference is to help the storyteller improve the story and gain fluency, skill, and confidence.

Calendars

I have included an outline teacher calendar and a "due dates" student calendar. Change the calendar to fit the schedule that works best for you and your students. I find that, working one long period a day, the whole unit takes about four weeks.

Working Tips

Keep students from memorizing if you can. They will do much better if they know the story "in their gut" and memorize only the beginning and any particularly good imagery. They need to know the sequence of events, the characters, and the settings really well.

You may want to help them work on distinct voices and/or rhythms for different characters. Be sure each child works with several partners and small groups as she rehearses and gives and receives responses.

Children in kindergarten and younger can sometimes become mesmerized by being "on stage," and it may be difficult for them to end their stories. A technique I have used to help them stick to the story is to divide a piece of drawing paper into three (folding works well) and ask each child to draw the beginning, the middle, and the end of his story. As the child tells the story, the teacher can hold the paper and move the child through each part: "Excellent. How well you told the beginning!" "And that's the middle of the story." "Very good! What a good ending!"

Storytelling Rules

Here are some rules to keep the storyteller feeling safe and in charge of her story:

1. The story belongs to the storyteller.

2. The kind of response the storyteller gets is defined by the storyteller.

3. The rehearsal partner's first comment should be specific praise ("I liked the way you made me feel the pine needles through my moccasins when we were going through the forest").

4. The requested response is specific and is stated positively.

5. The storyteller decides whether to accept or reject suggestions for changing the story or the ways she tells it (see #1).

Response requests are the result of a brainstorming session and they are specific. Post a list where everyone can see it and refer to it.

With each opportunity to tell the story to a rehearsal partner, a small group, or the whole class, for their specific response, the storyteller grows in confidence—and the story grows in depth. By the time the student is ready to tell the story as a finished piece, he knows he can do it—he already has.

Response Requests

Here are examples of some responses storytellers might request in their rehearsal conference. The best way to generate a list like this is to have your class brainstorm their own response requests and then post them where everyone can see them. One response—two at most—are enough for any telling.

1. Does the story flow?
2. Is the description good?
3. Can you "see" the story? Do you feel like you're "there"?
4. Is there any part that is not clear? Is there any place where I lose you?
5. Can you tell what the characters are really like?
6. Is there any place where there is too much information?
7. Is there any place where you need more information?
8. Can you tell who is talking?
9. Does the story grab you? Where and how?
10. Does the mood (or moods) come through?
11. What really works well? (What should *not* be changed?)
12. Is my vocabulary good?
13. Do I speak clearly?
14. Do I speak loudly enough?
15. Do I vary my speech?
16. Is my speech fluent? (no "uh," "ya know," or repeated "then," "like")

17. Do I use my body?
18. Do I use facial expression?
19. Do I use the space around me?
20. Does the beginning hook you into the story?
21. Is the conclusion satisfying?

Guided Imagery

A good way to help students visualize the setting is to take them on a mental journey using guided imagery. Ask them to close their eyes, and then to choose an interior (or exterior) setting for their story. Giving them time to see, feel, touch, smell, taste, and hear, talk to them quietly:

"You are standing in your setting. What surrounds you? What colors do you see? What shades? Is the air warm? cool? cold? What is the weather? Can you feel the sun on the back of your neck? What do you hear? Listen carefully. What is under your feet? Can you feel that? What do you smell? Are you hungry? Put your hand out and touch the nearest object. How does it feel under your fingers? . . ."

Or you can do a visualization based on a specific place:

"You are standing on the edge of a high cliff overlooking the ocean. The waves roll in and break with a thundering roar, sending silver spray high in the air. Smell the sea and the salt. Hear the gulls cry as they fly and glide above the shore, constantly searching for food. Feel the soft breeze in your face and hair . . ."

These are only examples. What is important is that the teacher also imagine and visualize along with the students. This will help the pacing and encourage students to do their own visualization as they prepare a story.

Learning Logs for Storytelling

The use of learning logs with storytelling is an idea I owe to Marni Schwartz, a storyteller, teacher, and colleague from the National Council of Teachers of English Committee on Storytelling (Schwartz 1989). She suggests that students keep a separate journal for their storytelling. In the first part they record their insights, discoveries, questions, rehearsal notes, and reactions to other storytellers' work. In the second part they keep synopses of stories they read, hear, or remember as they look for new stories to tell. If the stories are from a written source, they should include title and author, so they can give credit. Other sources are credited as well ("I heard this story from my grandmother, Mrs. Joan Smith"). This is good storytelling etiquette.

The two-part learning log provides students (and teacher) with a record of how they found the story, its development, and their own growth as a storyteller. It puts students in charge of their own learning.

Below is a list of suggested questions to get students thinking about storytelling. Use them one at a time and feel free to change them to fit your own purpose.

Choosing a Story

How are you going about choosing a story to tell?

Who or what is helping you choose your story?

What are some of your impressions after hearing this particular storyteller? (For example, more experienced students modeling, visiting tellers, videos, teacher, or fellow students.)

Where are you in terms of choosing: decided? undecided between two? in need of help?

What do you find in the story that makes you think it will be especially good to tell?

Will you have to cut the original version? Stretch it?

Learning a Story

How are you rehearsing at home: to an audience? to a wall? to a pet? in front of a mirror?

What is helping you learn your story?

Are your rehearsals different from each other? In what ways?

Have you taped your telling? Does listening to your tape help you visualize your story?

Does the story change as you tell it to friends, family, the teacher? Why do you think that is?

We've talked about the difference between memorizing and visualizing; how are you learning your story?

(After a class exercise, such as working on the charts or a session of guided imagery): How did this activity help/hinder your story preparation?

Is anything giving you trouble as you learn your story? What?

Polishing a Story

Does your story include conversation? Does your voice and how you use your body tell us who is talking?

Are you using your body and your facial expressions to become the characters in your story? Do you know them well enough to do this easily?

Are you remembering to make eye contact? With whom have you tried it? How does it feel?

Is your story set? Do you let yourself ad lib or are you set in wording and gestures?

Are you articulating clearly (speaking so your audience can follow every bit of your story)?

How about pace? Does the pace fit the story?

Whose rehearsal has impressed you? What is another teller doing that pulls you in?

During and After "Final" Tellings

Whose story left the biggest impression on you today? Why?

What image remains with you from a story told today? How did the teller make that image come alive for you?

What seems similar in the stories you've heard?

Do the best stories have anything in common? What?

Who added a technique that surprised you? What was it?

What went really well in telling your story? (Be generous with yourself, no false modesty.)

What will you do differently when you tell this story again?

Performance Opportunities

By the time your students have learned their stories and told them in the classroom to their peers, they will have worked long and hard. They deserve performance opportunities over and above that final "dress rehearsal"—telling the story to their classmates. Here are some suggestions for further venues:

- Invite other classes into your classroom for selected performances.

- Send your students to other classrooms to share their stories.

- Invite parents and other family members to an evening of stories.

- Arrange to have your students tell stories at another school.

- Consult your librarian and schedule storytelling in your school library.

- Ask your branch library if they will schedule student storytelling.

- Make arrangements to tell stories at retirement communities and nursing homes.

- Check with local radio stations that may welcome student storytellers on specific broadcasts.

- Look into community access television that may have a time slot for student storytellers.

Storytelling Across the Curriculum

Storytelling can be used in teaching subject matter all across the curriculum. A story you tell to entertain your students may also contain elements useful in multicultural applications, math, science, almost any subject you are teaching. Stories have a way of engaging the imagination. A hint from the teacher or from students can direct thinking toward applications that fit a specific lesson!

Storytelling and Science

Storytelling has an important role to play in teaching science. (The history and rationale for these applications can be found in Chapters 2 and 3.)

Scientific Method: Storytelling can lead students to an understanding of the basic philosophy of science: scientific method. What mysterious thing do scientists do that is so different and difficult? The answer is simple. They ask questions and try to solve them in an organized way.

1. Tell a story. Almost any story. Ask your students what else they want to know about that story.

2. Write their questions on the board. Be sure to accept all questions and write them all down. Wait to give time to the shy students.

3. Ask your students to categorize their questions.

4. Discuss which questions belong in each category (some may fit into more than one). Assign each question to the category or categories you and the class have decided are appropriate. Do you have all the questions in at least one category?

5. Ask the students to decide which category is most important and explore it first. Arrange the categories in order of priority.

6. Tell them a scientist can answer only one question at a time. Discuss which question is most important in category one, which is next most important, and so on.

7. Ask students how they are going to find the answer to the question. Record all the information they come up with on the chalkboard. Be sure to ask them to give reasons for their experimental designs. These are hypotheses. When you have a handful of hypotheses for your question, you are ready for the next step.

8. Discuss the projected experiments and decide which is likely to be most useful in answering your question.

9. Emphasize to students the importance of keeping accurate records of what they do and of their observations.

10. Impress upon them the importance of replicating their experiments and be sure they understand why this is necessary. If they carry out the experiments, ask a different group of students to try to replicate them.

When you have finished, you will have walked them through scientific method—even if you haven't done the experiments. They will have

- identified several problems
- categorized them
- thought of possible answers to their questions (hypotheses)
- designed experiments
- figured out which experiments to do first and why
- drawn conclusions based on experimental data
- kept records of what they have done and what they intend to do
- understood the importance of replicability.

A Specific Experiment: Suppose you want your students to investigate the properties of a gooey material, something like play dough or

Slime. You might well tell them *Bartholomew and the Oobleck* by Dr. Seuss and ask them what else they want to know about oobleck. When you have listed all the questions, ask students to put them in categories (this is like "scientific method"). Next, arrange the categories and questions in order of importance and ask them how they will go about finding the answers. Have them design the experiments they are going to undertake. Be sure to remind them to observe carefully, take notes on their experiments, and repeat each experiment so they know it is replicable.

As they report on their results, ask what conclusions they came to. Be sure they can cite the experimental data that led to these conclusions.

Original Stories: You can create stories to fit your purpose. "Storm!" and "Bubbles and Paper Towels" (found in Appendix A) are both examples.

Scientific Terms: Naming is an important aspect of science. Scientific terms and names are important because they contain *meaning*. Stories emphasize this point for students. Tell "Rumpelstiltskin," for example. The power of knowing the name is what saves the queen's child. In many ancient and Native American myths, naming an object creates that object.

Science in Nature: Well-researched, scientifically accurate children's stories about flora and fauna are naturals for storytelling. Tell some of these stories to your students. The story form carries the information you want them to learn, and they will remember it far better than facts on a worksheet or in a lecture. If the students do the research and turn the information they learn into stories to tell, that knowledge becomes internalized, part of their intellectual fabric.

Ecology and Environmental Issues: Use Earth Day celebrations as a showcase for students' stories about the environment. Encourage recycling in school by telling recycling stories. (See Appendix B for resources.)

Stories and Research: With your students, brainstorm a list of natural phenomena (for example, rain, rainbows, lightning, thunder, the metamorphosis of insects, the ripening of fruit). Have your students create and tell myths to explain a particular phenomenon. Then group students by subject and have them research the scientific explanation for that phenomenon.

Stories That Feature the Scientific Method: Tell stories in which the protagonist uses scientific method to solve a problem. Examples of this can be found in almost any mystery story! The best known detective is probably Sherlock Holmes. *Encyclopedia Brown* is a good model for younger students.

Men and Women in Science: There are wonderful stories about scientists and scientific discoveries. Whether told by the teacher/storyteller or by students who have chosen this means of sharing their projects, stories personalize scientific information so that it immediately becomes more available and more memorable.

Life Lessons in Stories: Many science stories contain valuable life messages for students. Good scientists do experiment after experiment, testing hypotheses. They do not quit after one or two failures. They learn from their failures. Scientists may have to defend their ideas in the face of criticism. It may be years before new ideas are accepted. This was certainly true of Pasteur's theory that microbes caused illness.

Ethics: Tell the true stories of ethical problems scientists face. Have your students debate these problems or hold a mock trial and have the jury (class) decide the issue.

Review Information Previously Taught: Challenge your students to choose some aspect of a science unit you are teaching and improvise a story using the information they have discovered. Give them three minutes each to tell their stories to each other in pairs. Then ask some of them to share their stories with the class. Students may wish to write down or record their stories following this exercise as part of their learning experience.

Evaluation: Have your students use story as an alternative to a standard end-of-unit test to evaluate what they have learned. This is a written rather than an oral story. The written stories can be added to student portfolios and told later to the class.

Storytelling and Math

Storytelling is also useful in mathematics where it can help students think mathematically and understand the world of math. Here are some intersections of storytelling and math I have discovered. (You will find the history and rationale for these applications in Chapters 2 and 4.)

Math Is Everywhere: Tell your students a story and ask them to look for the math applications. Tell "Rapunzel," for example. They are likely to ask about how high the tower was, how long Rapunzel's hair was, whether it was braided or loose and how that affected its length, how strong her hair was braided and loose, how much the old crone weighed, how much the prince weighed, and so on.

Have students work in pairs on problems based on their own questions, exchange problems with other student pairs, and work on solutions. The fact that students have created their own problems will motivate their work on the solutions.

Mathematical Stories: Some stories have a specific mathematical application. Tell these stories to illustrate a mathematical principal. These include counting rhymes and stories, stories of halving and doubling, large and small numbers, all four basic operations, fractions, geometry, powers, and many other math disciplines.

Word Problems Are Stories: Challenge your students to create their own word problems. The partner or group listening to the story can do mental arithmetic to solve the problem, or if you prefer, they can do paper and pencil solutions.

Venn Diagrams: Teach the concept of Venn diagrams by using different versions of stories. Ask students what version of a well known story they know (for example, "Alladin"). Ask them to list the principal elements of the story on strips of paper. Then tell them a different version of the same story. Again, ask them to list the principal elements on strips of paper. Now ask them to arrange the elements common to both versions in the space between the two groups of paper strips. Give them pieces of yarn and have them circle the important elements of each version. The result will be a Venn diagram. Venn diagrams show overlapping elements in math, both similarities and differences.

Math History: Tell stories of mathematical discoveries. Students will remember information far better than they would after a lecture or a reading assignment with comprehension questions to answer.

Biographies of Mathematicians: Tell stories of the lives and times of mathematicians. Can mathematics get you into political trouble? Tell your students Gallileo's story. His mathematical proof that the earth moved, that it travelled around the sun, put his life in jeopardy with the Inquisition. Your students learn math and history at the same time!

Students Report Using Stories: If your students report on individual projects to the class, storytelling is a powerful way for them to share their discoveries. Creating and telling the story will solidify that knowledge for both teller and listeners.

Teachers' Original Stories: Create and tell your own stories to challenge your students to think mathematically or to motivate their exploration of a particular math discipline (estimation, measurement, powers . . .).

Students' Original Stories: Have students create and tell stories that contain math ideas. Let other students find the math and structure the problems. These stories can be developed as part of their language arts classes. Students can tell the stories during math period and ask their peers to do the problems (variation of *Word Problems Are Stories*).

Storytelling and Language Arts
Storytelling is right at home with language arts (see Chapter 2 for a full discussion of the rationale). Storytelling addresses the neglected arts of listening and speaking. Developmentally, a child listens and hears, and then speaks. Writing and reading come later. Through storytelling, the child hears stories being told before he tells stories. The first stories a student tells in this unit are short, informal pieces, parts of storytelling games, and anecdotes out of his own experience. Storytelling encourages children to speak clearly and distinctly.

Students go on to read as they do research and to write. They also learn to summarize when they use storytelling charts and when they tell others about their stories. They learn about how to create and develop characters and moods and settings. And they learn to exercise their imaginations, something that is becoming increasingly important as the imposed images of television take over whole generations.

Language arts often provides a framework for other disciplines. The subject matter of storytelling is often the stuff of other disciplines. As such storytelling also has applications across the curriculum.

Storytelling and Social Studies

Here are some ways to apply storytelling to social studies:

Stories of History: You, as teacher, can tell stories to make history come alive and to put your students on the scene of real historical events. A careful reading of your social studies textbook or a good encyclopedia will unearth rich material, and further research will allow you to incorporate authentic details.

For example, re-create the Boston Massacre for your study of the American Revolution. It wasn't a massacre, but a street fight, more like a brawl. Look at a street map and pictures of Boston at the time. Consider the weather on March 5, 1770. It was probably cold and miserable. Tell the story from the point of view of a colonial bystander about the age of your students. British soldiers were standing guard. Fifty or sixty colonists were taunting them. Finally, under extreme provocation, the soldiers fired into the crowd. It was a frightening incident for a nine-year-old to witness. Five colonists died and Sam Adams turned the events to his own use—fomenting rebellion.

Students Report Research: Have students tell stories as the culminating project of their research in a particular unit. History and culture come alive for them and become integral to their knowledge. If they tell their stories well, the information they impart will also be internalized by classmates who are listening to the story.

Multicultural Applications: Tell your students stories from other cultures and encourage them to research and tell stories like these. This will help them truly understand the culture they are studying from the inside. (Note the caution about using folktales for multicultural education in Chapter 2.)

Family Stories: Students—and teacher—can research and tell stories about their own families and cultures. This is a wonderful way to help students understand the richness and diversity of our society.

When family stories are your focus, there are several additional steps. Students need to be trained as interviewers, and parents need to be alerted and reassured. The individuals being interviewed can always refuse to answer specific questions. The interviewer respects their privacy.

1. Role-play interviews. Remind students that good manners are essential ("please" and "thank you" are appropriate).

2. Have them set up a time to conduct the interview that is convenient for the interviewee. The optimum time for successful interviewing of family members may be over a holiday, such as Thanksgiving, when families get together. You may wish to schedule your unit on family storytelling to take advantage of such a holiday.

3. Interview parents, grandparents, oldest available family member. (Long distance telephone calls are not a good way to interview. Much of the story emerges in the interviewee's mannerisms, gestures, and facial expression.) Elderly neighbors and friends are also wonderful subjects. In the case of divided families, students should choose the person they want to interview.

4. Here are a few starter questions. You and your class can come up with others:

   Who was the first person on your side of the family to come to America?
   When and why did he or she come?
   Where did he or she come from and where did he or she settle?
   What was school like when you were in my grade?
   What games did you play? How were they played?
   What was the most exciting thing that ever happened to you?
   What was the scariest thing that ever happened to you?
   What was the most embarrassing thing that ever happened to you?
   What family stories do you know? (This can open a whole trunkful.)
   What stories do you know about me when I was little?

5. Emphasize the importance of pursuing a subject further. Follow-up questions often trigger the memory of additional details.

Please tell me more about . . .
What happened then?
Who else was involved?

"How" and "Why" questions will also elicit more information.

6. Students should be sure to arrange a time to tell the person they interviewed their story.

7. When students have researched, chosen, and rehearsed their stories, and performed them for the class, you may wish to have them tell their stories to others. (See p. 73 for suggestions of places and audiences for student performances.)

Storytelling and English as a Second Language
Storytelling is an integral part of many cultures. Your ESL students may be well accustomed to hearing and telling stories. When you work with students whose first language is not English, it is helpful if these students tell their story in their primary language first and then in English. This gives everyone an opportunity to hear the language of another country and celebrates the unique language ability of the ESL student.

Exercises
Adapt these exercises to your own teaching style and to the ages and needs of your students.

Warm-ups
Touch a Star: Stand in a circle. Teacher says, "Reach as high as you can. Can your fingers touch a star? Reach. Reach. Stretch every part from your toes to your fingertips."

The Seed: Teacher says, "Make yourself as small as possible. Curl up into a seed. You are resting, sleeping, deep in the earth. It is dark and safe. Rain falls and softens the ground. You stir. The sun warms the earth and you begin to grow slowly, slowly. Feel yourself grow, gently uncurling. A little tendril breaks through the earth. Feel the sun. Feel the gentle rain. Grow. Sway gently in the wind."

Move to the Beat: Teacher gives directions for students to spread out so that each person has space to move but doesn't interfere with anyone else. Teacher can clap, hit a book with the flat of her hand, play a drum. She should vary the beat from slow to fast and back, to syncopated, and so on. End with a slow beat.

Shake the Tree: Teacher says, "Look at this big apple tree. Do you see all those ripe, juicy apples hanging from the tree? You can pick them! Reach high for that crimson one. Shake the tree. Pick up what falls to the ground . . . Wait a minute. Something has happened here. The apple tree is changing. It has become a money tree. The biggest bills are at the top. (Activity increases.) Reach! Reach! Can you jump for that thousand dollar bill? Oh, it's gone. The money tree has disappeared."

Stretch and Freeze: Students move during a drum beat and then freeze in position when the drum beat stops or is especially loud—an exercise like "statues." The teacher controls the movement and may call out an object for students to become when they freeze (a bird, a skyscraper, a TV).

Stretch and Freeze with a Partner: Stretch and freeze and end up touching one other person.

Positions 1-2-3-4: Teacher calls position numbers. 1, hands together over head; 2, hands on hips; 3, hands at sides; 4, palms flat on floor. Vary the pace.

Vocal Warm-ups: Say an ordinary phrase ("How are you?" "I'm going to the mall," "Please pick up the mail") in different ways: loud or soft tones, angry or happy feelings, old or young voices. The teacher provides settings and directions.

Sing Vowel Sounds: Varying from soft to loud, try to help your students breathe from their diaphragms. The school music teacher can help with this and suggest other vocal warm-ups.

Theatre Games

Telephone, or Pass the Message: Students sit in a circle. The teacher explains, "The object of the game is to get the secret message all the way around the circle unchanged. To do this you must whisper clearly and listen carefully. If you don't understand the message when it is whispered to you, you may say 'Operator?' and the person passing the message to you will repeat it. Everyone must be very quiet so that the message can be heard and understood." Hint: Keep the message simple. Have the students explain why this is an important game for storytelling.

Roll the Ball: Roll an imaginary ball across the circle from person to person. Make sure everyone gets included. No talking is allowed. Students must focus on the imaginary ball to "see" where it goes and be ready when it comes to them. If the ball leaves the ground, it disappears and the game ends.

Pass the Object: Sit in a circle. Hold an imaginary object in your hands (for example, a banana.) Feel the weight and the shape, see the color, and so on. Mime how the object is used. Pass it to the next person (no talking). That person shows he understands what the object is by using it appropriately, then changes the object to something else (a book? a typewriter? a toothbrush?), shows how the new object works, and passes it to the next person in the circle. A mime exercise.

Tug-O-War: In pairs, or in two teams, students play tug-o-war, but the line and the rope are imaginary. This is a mime exercise, one that uses the whole body. Students must work together for the exercise to be successful. Cooperative mime.

Mirrors: Children pair up. One leads in making slow movements. The other follows her exactly, trying for simultaneous movement. The object is for the partners to concentrate and focus so well, it is difficult for observers to tell who is leading. Switch roles. As students become more skilled at this, the pace and complexity of movement can increase.

Charades: One person or team leaves the room. Those remaining decide on a saying, story, book, movie, TV show, or song title. The person or team comes back into the room. Those who know the secret message act out words or syllables without speaking, while the other players guess.

Mime Exercises: Teacher verbally creates an imaginary setting. Students act out their (silent) response to whatever environment the teacher has created. Examples: standing in the playground on the first snowy day, crossing a busy street, picking berries in a blackberry patch, kicking a can across an empty lot.

Storytelling Games

Mixed-Up Fairy Tales: Each student gets two slips of blank paper. On one he writes the title of a well-known fairy tale (for example, Cinderella, Little Red Riding Hood). On the second he writes a question about that fairy tale or another one. The question can be silly or out of the classical context of the story ("Who was Cinderella's dress designer?" "What happened to Cinderella and the Prince after the wedding?").

Collect the slips separately, titles (shuffled) in one box or basket, questions (shuffled) in another. Pass the two baskets around the circle and ask each person to take one slip from each container (one title and one question). Give students two minutes to create a story based on the title and the question. Take turns telling the stories. The first time you play, the teacher should go first to model how it is done. Afterwards the teacher can go last because the students will know exactly what to do and will be eager to tell their own mixed-up fairy tales.

Story Places: This is a storytelling version of charades. The storyteller takes the name of a town, state, or country and weaves the syllables into a story. The storyteller can be asked to shorten a story or change it on a second or third telling. The stories can be simple or quite elaborate. Listeners must guess the place name. (For example: "I woke up very late this morning because the alarm didn't go off. The *boss* was furious and when I finally got to the office there was a *ton* of work waiting for me" (*Boston*).

Fortunately . . . but Unfortunately . . . : This game is a cooperative story that goes around the circle. Anyone (first time the teacher) can begin. She starts the story and has it well launched before saying, "But unfortunately . . ." and then the story goes to the next person. That person adds something unfortunate to the story and ends with "but fortunately . . ." and so the story progresses around the circle. Remind your students that the story should have a cohesive beginning, middle, and end and that the last tellers are responsible for bringing about a good ending. This game promotes careful, cooperative work as well as listening, thinking, and speaking.

Variation of Fortunately . . . Unfortunately . . . : Begin a story with one sentence. Each person in the circle then adds a sentence, all working toward completing the story by the time the last person in the circle has contributed. If the group is small, the story may go around two or three times.

Another Variation of Fortunately . . . Unfortunately . . . :   Roll a ball from person to person in the circle but in no particular pattern (perhaps only the teacher rolls the ball). The person who receives the ball adds the next part of the story. Be sure everyone gets a chance to be the ball receiver/storyteller.

Talking Stick: Pass a stick from person to person around the circle. Whoever holds the stick has the floor. That person may add to the story, tell his own story, or choose to remain silent by passing the stick on to the next person. This is based on a Native American custom (Jacobson 1993).

Point of View: Tell a familiar story from an unusual point of view. Each student gets a slip of paper with the name of a familiar story and the character from whose point of view the story is to be told. Allow a couple of minutes for students to think. Teacher can model the first time. Examples:

Story	*Other Points of View*
"Cinderella"	stepmother
	either stepsister
	father
	prince
	fairy godmother
"Little Red Riding Hood"	wolf
	grandmother
	hunter

New Last Name: This is a version of Grandmother's Trunk. Each student in the circle chooses a new last name, just for now, that represents something he really wants to be. Example: Suzie Horserider, Joe Fisherman, Betty TV Star, Mike Environmentalist. Each student must repeat all the names from the beginning and then add his own new name. Teacher is first or last.

Variation of New Last Name: Each person chooses a new last name and, as that person, tells a brief story of an incident in the future.

Sound Effects: On separate slips of paper write different sound effects: squeaky door, thunder, bears, hissing or slithering snake, cats fighting, and so on. Pass these out. Each student, in turn, makes the sound until the others guess what it is. No props.

Say the Phrase: Pass out slips of paper on which you have written the name of an emotion: anger, love, hatred, delight, wonder, embarrassment, and so on. Students then say a neutral phrase while exhibiting that emotion. For example, "Hello, how are you?" "Excuse me," "When, tomorrow?"

Student Guide Sheets
Storytelling

Name _____

Storytelling is as old as humankind. Through every age people have told stories: to entertain, to teach and to learn, to pass history and customs from one generation to the next, to boast, to illustrate an idea.

We are all going to tell stories. What follows is an outline of what you will be doing. We'll go over it carefully together and you will see that you have a number of choices to make and steps to follow. Everyone will tell stories, and you will help each other become really good storytellers. Here's how it will go:

Choices:
I. Think about your audience.
   A. For whom will you be telling your story? Has your audience been assigned? If yes, skip to section B.
   What age level is your audience?

1. Kindergarten	6. Fifth grade
2. First grade	7. Sixth grade
3. Second grade	8. Older grades
4. Third grade	9. Adults
5. Fourth grade	10. Mixed audience of children and adults

   B. What is your audience interested in?
   You can find out by

   1. Asking the audience what kinds of stories they like.
   2. Looking through books at the appropriate level—teachers and librarian will help.
   3. Remembering what you liked when you were that age.

II. Choose a story to tell. Is the type of story assigned? If yes, find a story of that genre (type).
   A. Choose a story you already know, research and tell a family story, create an original story, find a story in the library.
   B. Other kinds of stories to consider:

1. Animal story	5. Folk tale
2. Fairy tale	6. Ghost story
3. Adventure story	7. Fantasy story
4. Myth	8. Family story

   9. Some other kind of story. What _____?

III. If you are choosing a story from the library, read many different stories—perhaps as many as two dozen. The story you choose should be one that shouts "Tell me!" to you. You're going to work long and hard to make the story yours. It needs to be one you really want to tell!

Learn Your Story:

Now that you have decided on your story and made all those decisions, here's what happens next:

I. Become thoroughly familiar with the story—even if it's one you have created. *Don't memorize it* but get to know it so well you could start anywhere and tell it. Start by summarizing the story, out loud, to yourself or a conference partner. Tell the story in two or three sentences. Use one or more of the processes described below. Be sure to check with me so we can decide together which process will work best for you.
   A. Draw the story. Use color. Get the details in and think about smells, textures, sounds. Tell the pictures.
   B. Storytelling Charts

      1. Chart I: The Story. Divide the story into three or four principal parts.
         a. Write the names of the characters who appear in the first part in the column headed "Characters."
         b. In the column headed "Action" describe in as few words as possible what happens in the first part of the story.
         c. Find one or two words to describe the mood of that first part of the story. Write that in the column headed "Emotion."

      d. Under images write phrases that paint the pictures you see in your head as you visualize the story. Don't forget the colors, sounds, smells, tastes, textures.

      e. Fill in the rest of the chart for each part of the story.

2. Chart II: Characters. This chart will help you get to know your characters really well. The better you know your characters, the better your audience will know them too.

      a. List characters by name.

      b. Describe each character physically. Be sure to include age, coloring, size, shape, movement, and so on. What is your first impression of this character? Do you have a strong image?

      c. What most interests each character? What is her job or principal occupation? Does she enjoy what she does? How about her family and friends?

      d. Try to think of a phrase or a gesture that typifies each character. Maybe he keeps asking "Why?" or maybe his laugh is really distinctive.

Knowing all of these things about your characters will help you portray them as distinct people when you tell your story. You may also want to draw or paint each of your characters. If you do, be sure you show each one doing something typical.

3. Chart III: Setting. Learn all about your setting. Take a trip, in your imagination, to each of the places in your story. See colors, shapes, light. Hear sounds. Feel textures. Smell the air. Taste the food. Use this information in the third chart. Again, you may want to draw or paint your scenes but be sure to include what you know about all those other senses.

C. Web your story. Be sure your web includes all the important components—plot, characters, setting—with details. Again, the more you know, the better your audience will be able to be there with you when you tell your story.

Rehearsals:

A. Tell your story to yourself. Add details that use the important information you've discovered. See if you can find a "voice," a physical stance, or a gesture for each character.

B. Thinking time again. Go back to your charts: Close your eyes and imagine each scene. What do you see? Are there pictures and other sensations? There should be. Can you add the mental pictures to your story? These are the images that help your story come to life.

C. Tell yourself the story again. Tell the pictures. Are the images there? Which ones feel right? Which ones seem to belong in your story? Keep those.

D. Tell the story to yourself again. Do your characters have distinct personalities? Does that come out when you describe them, when they speak and move?

E. When you feel ready, have a conference. Tell your partner what response you want. Tell your story. Listen to the response. What really works? Is the response helpful? What will you do about it? Remember, it's *your* story. *You* decide whether the response is helpful.

F. Have another conference with another partner. Ask for a different response. Repeat the process. Remember, you and your story are growing together each time you tell it.

G. Be sure that each time you tell your story you credit the author or source of the story: "This story comes from a book by Arnold Lobel called *Ming Lo Moves the Mountain*," or "This is a story my grandmother, Mrs. Jane Smith, told me," or "This is an original story."

H. Tell your story to your teacher, then to the class.

I. Now do your scheduled performance—and good luck! You'll be great!

J. Make an audiotape of your story. Listen to it. Isn't it great? (These last two are interchangeable.)

Important information: There are NO mistakes. It's your story and the way you tell it is right for you. If you leave out important information, say "Oh, did I remember to tell you that . . ."

Student Schedule

Here is your schedule. Fill in the due dates as I give them to you. Decisions, decisions:

1. Type of story _____ due _____

2. Audience _____ due _____

3. Original story or published one? _____

   Title _____

   Author _____

   Due _____

4. Time for library or family research, including weekends _____

5. Preparation time:

   Pictures due _____

   Web due _____

   Chart I due _____

   Chart II due _____

   Chart III due _____

Rehearse, confer, rehearse, confer, rehearse, confer, rehearse!

6. Taped performance (title) _____ due _____

7. Performance for class, with feedback (scheduled date) _____

8. Evaluation. Due _____

These dates are the latest. Early birds are always welcome!

Storytelling Chart I

Name _____

Due _____

Part	Characters	Actions	Emotions	Images (pictures)

Storytelling Chart II: Characters

Character	Describe looks, coloring, stature, etc.	Interests/jobs	Personality: habits, key phrase, gesture

Storytelling Chart III: Setting

Place	Weather, season time, terrain	Colors	Shapes and textures	Smells and tastes	Sounds

Web Your Story

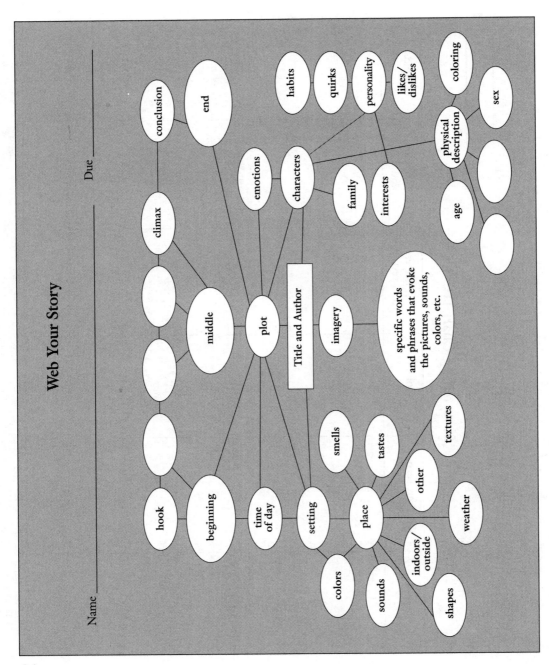

Name _____   Due _____

Suggested Teacher Calendar

This calendar is a general outline only. You may wish to spend more time having your students find or create their stories, or, if the stories are content oriented doing the research needed. This calendar is designed for stories that will be told in formal performance. Casual improvisational storytelling, the kind that so often happens in teaching science and math, goes very quickly, with no initial preparation and rehearsal.

1. Type of story _____   Due Day 1 or 2

2. Audience _____   Due Day 1 or 2

3. Original story or published one _____   Due Day 1 or 2
or following
library trip

4. Time for library trip, interviews, or other research.   Days 3–5

5. Preparation time: Pictures: Day 5 or 6

6. Preparation time: Story web: Day 5 or 6

7. Preparation time: Storytelling Chart I: Days 7–9
Characters, sequence, imagery

8. Preparation time: Storytelling Chart II: Days 10–11
Characterization

9. Preparation time: Storytelling Chart III: Days 11–12
Setting(s), guided imagery

10. Rehearse, rehearse, rehearse—with a variety of response
partners—about a week.   Days 13–17

11. Taped story_____   Due Days
17/18

12. Performance for class with feedback: When
scheduled

13. Evaluation   Following
performance

Sample Letter to Parents About Family Stories

_____ School

Date_____

Dear Parents:

As we learn more about American history, it is time for the children to begin to research their own family histories. Each of us, no matter how "ordinary," is unique, and each American family or visiting family is part of our history. We have all made contributions to America. Discovering their family's experiences makes history come alive for children.

I would like each child to learn about his or her family origins and to hear as many family stories or anecdotes as you can help them find. (We are really not interested in family trees.) Since holiday time is when families traditionally get together, please help your child arrange a time to get family stories rolling. Interviews can be with one individual at a time or when the whole family is together. The students have brainstormed questions to ask you and other family members. A tape recorder can be a great help to your child in gathering these stories. Attic and storeroom searches and photograph albums are good places to discover family stories.

I am most grateful for your help and cooperation. We do not wish to be intrusive or to embarrass anyone. Please feel free to tell your child that you do not wish to answer a particular question if it concerns information you do not want to share. On the other hand, you are a wonderful resource for your children and for our Social Studies unit.

If you have questions, please drop me a note and I will be glad to call you in the evening or set up a conference time. Thank you for your time, effort, and cooperation.

Sincerely yours,

- -

Please sign and send back this tear-off sheet so that I know you have received this letter. Thank you.

I received the letter about family histories.

Parent Signature _____

Comments:

Self-Evaluation for Storyteller

Name _____

Date _____

Title _____

This is the _____ time I've told this story.

Audience (grade level, number of listeners) _____

Did you speak clearly? _____

      Yes   *No*

Pace

_____

Too Fast   *Just right*   *Too slow*

Were you "into" the story, and was the audience with you?

_____

Very effective   *Disaster*

Audience reaction:

_____

Glued in place   *Itchy*

How could you do an even better performance? _____

Do you want to try again? _____

What audience this time? _____

Make an appointment (date and time) _____

Rehearse _____

Listener Evaluation Sheet

Date _____

Storyteller _____

Story title _____

Check along the line where you think the check mark belongs:

The story was:

_____
Wonderful   *Only so-so*

_____
Too short   *Just right*   *Too long*

The storyteller was:

_____
Super-duper   *Not quite ready*

Suggestions for the storyteller:

Would you like the storyteller to return sometime?

Other ideas?

Afterword

"But I have so much to do and this sounds like a lot of work! I don't have time to become a storyteller, let alone take a month of school time to teach my students to tell stories!"

It is true that teaching and learning storytelling takes time. But there are many payoffs.

If you encourage your students to work together and support each other, that kind of experience will help make them a community of independent learners. At the same time, it will make your life simpler. It will free you to work with individuals, encourage small groups, keep tabs on progress in your classroom, and work on your own storytelling.

As students learn storytelling, they practice all the language skills, and they learn the science or math or social studies content. Storytelling is a powerful teaching/learning method with applications all across the curriculum. (Does all this sound familiar?)

We all know that no one way works well for every student. People learn in different ways. We know something about teaching and learning styles. I don't advocate storytelling as your only teaching method, nor do I believe that it will transform every student into a brilliant scholar or even a brilliant storyteller. But storytelling is an effective tool, and we can hardly afford to ignore any effective teaching method, especially one that demystifies and motivates students in the vital areas of science and mathematics. So use this book, try your hand at storytelling, and have a wonderful time.

Let me end with a traditional story, "Truth and Parable":

Once upon a time Truth, naked Truth, went about the streets of the town. Wherever he went, people avoided him. If they saw him coming, they crossed to the other side of the street. If he knocked on a door, people opened the door a crack and then slammed it shut in his face. He wandered cold and sad and lonely through the town.

Parable came upon him. She was decked out in bright colors; in satins and silks, ribbons and laces.

"Friend Truth," she cried. "Why are you so sad?"

"Oh," Truth replied. "People scorn me. They do everything they can to avoid me. It must be because I am so old."

"That cannot be the reason," Parable returned. "They welcome me wherever I go and I am as old as you. I have an idea. Come with me. "

She took him to her house and there she opened a trunk. Brightly colored satins and velvets poured from the trunk: purple, red, emerald green, and fairest blue. She decked him out bravely and ever since, Truth and Parable have gone together, hand in hand, and they are welcomed wherever they go!

Appendix A
Stories

Storm!
by Barbara Lipke

"Come on, Jose! This is all new to me. I want you to show me everything!" Donna started out the door.

"Wait up! What shoes do you have on? I need to get my canteen and some food if we're going to be gone all day." Jose's thoughts were never far from food.

"Here are your sandwiches," said Jose's mother. "Watch the weather, Jose. A storm could come up."

"I know." Jose stuffed the generous bag of sandwiches into his backpack. He hung the canteen from his belt. "Thanks, Mom." He let the screen door of the convenience store bang shut behind him, dodged around the gas pumps, and looked for Donna. She had started down the road.

"Not that way!" Jose shouted to her. "This way!" They walked around the back of the three small buildings that made up the community and started toward the mesa that didn't seem far off.

In the morning light the mesa was umber against the cloudless blue sky. The sandy ground sloped upward toward the base. To Donna it seemed as though they were setting off across a trackless waste.

"Why did we turn?" she asked.

"We're following the trail."

"What trail? I don't see any trail!" She was accustomed to streets and sidewalks, and the Arizona desert was exciting and strange, like TV or a movie.

"Are there snakes?"

"Nah. Not usually. They get out of the way."

"Are there caves up there? I saw a movie where some kids got lost in a cave. What would happen if we got lost in a cave?"

Jose did not answer. This cousin had just come from New York for a visit. She was older. She was nice but she didn't seem to know much. He turned around and glanced at her feet. She was wearing thongs!

"Maybe we should go back and you can put on some real shoes."

"These are fine. They're what I wear when I go to the beach. The sand runs right out of them. All the kids wear them back east." Her tone implied that she knew and she'd help him understand how things are in the city, in civilization, and when you're older. An eleven-year-old boy can't be expected to know everything, she thought. But he's OK. I'll help him.

As they walked on, the mesa didn't seem any closer. The sun rose and it got hot. The face of the mesa turned yellow.

"How far away is that mesa? Are we going to climb it? Boy, it sure isn't getting closer."

"Yeah. It is. It's only about a mile."

They hiked on. Close up the mesa was a lot higher than it seemed from the house.

"It's hot. It gets hot in New York, but different. I'm thirsty. Can I have some water?"

"Yeah, sure. But only take a swallow or two. That's our water supply for the day." He stopped and held out the canteen.

"Isn't there any place else to get water?"

"No."

"Do you have a cup?"

"No. You just drink from the canteen."

"Oooh! Gross!"

Jose looked away.

"I'm sorry. I didn't mean to be like that. It's just what we say in the city. It's a joke."

"OK."

The sun beat down. Their shadows shortened.

"Boy! It's hot. Like an oven. Not even a breeze. Isn't there any shade?"

"See that dark line ahead on the mesa?" Jose pointed to a perpendicular line.

"Where? That? What's that?"

"That's the entrance to a canyon. There'll be shade there."

The dark line grew wider as they approached it. Then they were at the entrance of the canyon.

"Where does this canyon go? Does it go through the whole mesa?"

"No. It's a dead end. Sometimes, if it's rained a lot, a little water comes down over the edge at the far end. Not today."

They walked into the narrow canyon. It was cooler out of the sun but the air didn't stir. Even at noon, there was little direct sun. A narrow river of sunlight ran down the sloping floor of the canyon. The walls on both sides rose almost sheer. The sky was a deep violet-blue at the top of the walls.

Donna and Jose stood in the shade and looked.

"It's like New York, sort of. I mean, if you walk down the streets the buildings go up to the sky like this, sort of."

"Do you want to eat now?" Jose asked. He was always ready to eat.

"Oh. I want to explore the whole canyon. All the way. Can we do that first?"

"All right. We can at least walk down a way. There's a place with some rocks where we can sit and eat."

They walked down the canyon floor. A breeze stirred. The light changed. The river of sunlight disappeared. Jose looked up. The sky had lost its blue. Thunderheads piled up across the narrow space.

"Ow! The sand is stinging my legs," Donna said.

A rain drop plopped in the sand ahead of them. Jose felt another on his head.

"Come on, Donna! We've gotta get out of here!" Jose started back toward the mouth of the canyon. He caught his breath. A sick feeling clutched his stomach. They had come much further than he had thought.

"Why? It's just a little rain. I'm so hot it'll be nice to cool off." She opened her mouth to catch the rain drops. "I don't mind getting wet."

Dust devils started up all across the canyon floor.

"Ouch! Hey, that's not just sand. There're stones hitting me! Ow!"

"Come on, Donna, run! There's going to be a flood. We can get trapped here!"

It was raining hard now. There was a flash of lightning and thunder shook the walls of the canyon. The rain drove down stinging and beating them. They were soaked through.

Jose ran back and grabbed Donna's hand. He started to pull her toward the entrance to the canyon, back the way they had come.

"Ow! Ouch! There're stones in my thongs. I can't run!"

"Come on!"

Then he heard it: a roaring sound that drowned out the rain and thunder.

"Hurry, Donna. No. No. It's coming this way! Quick!" Still pulling her, he started up the side of the canyon. The wind was a solid wall they had to push through. Jose stumbled over rocks. He couldn't see through the blinding rain. Maybe there was a ledge where they'd be safe from the flood.

Donna hung back. "I can't! I can't!"

Jose pushed her in front of him. The cliff was uneven. There! The wind blew the rain aside and for a moment Jose saw a hole, a niche, just over there. He pushed Donna toward it!

The roaring grew closer. He glanced behind for a second. The canyon floor that had been a river of sunlit sand was a screaming, thundering torrent of water and rocks.

The niche was narrow, barely big enough for Donna. The ledge beside it crumbled. Jose pushed Donna up into the niche.

"Climb!" he ordered. It was a natural chimney. Narrow, closed, but maybe a way out. Maybe at least above the flood!

"Climb!" he screamed again.

"I can't! I don't know how!"

Jose pushed her up somehow. His heart pounded in his ears. Donna was wedged into the chimney. He climbed up behind her, pushing her feet with his head and hands.

Inside the chimney there was a different sound. The roaring echoed from a different direction. The wind pushed in at their feet. Suddenly Donna was gone. Jose climbed frantically, felt himself lifted, pushed, pulled up, up into the chimney.

When he opened his eyes he was lying on the ground, soaked to the skin, sore, confused. He lifted his head. He was—where? On the top of the mesa? Donna stirred nearby. The roaring was distant. A few random raindrops fell.

Overhead, thunderheads raced away to the east. The sun shone and a rainbow hung in the pale blue sky.

Use this story for lessons about

Air currents
Weather
Desert ecology
Thunder
Lightning (electricity)
Erosion
Flash floods
Permeability of soil
Waterpower
Rainbows
Light spectrum
Optics
Color perception
Shadows
Sounds as clues
Hearing

Bubbles and Paper Towels
by Barbara Lipke

I

"Sheila, I have an appointment with the eye doctor tomorrow. I'll be gone about an hour, maybe longer. Do you think you could take care of yourself and baby-sit Billy? Do you feel OK about baby-sitting?"

"Me? I can baby-sit?"

"Yes. I think you're old enough and you're responsible. How do you feel about it?"

"Oh yes, Mom. I can do it!"

That night, as she got ready for bed, Sheila thought about her new responsibilities. She was big enough to baby-sit. There was only one other girl in fourth grade who took care of younger brothers and sisters.

The next day in school, when Janet asked if Sheila could come over and play, Sheila explained that she couldn't; that she had to baby-sit Billy. Janet and the other girls had understood right away how important it was.

Sheila hurried home after school. Mother was ready to leave.

"You know the rules: no going off the block, call Daddy at the office if there's an emergency—and I've left the doctor's telephone number by the phone. It's a beautiful day and you two can play outside. You have your key, don't you?"

Sheila nodded and held up the key that hung on a shoelace around her neck. She felt very grown up!

"Mrs. Strawn is home if you really need her. She rests a lot in the afternoon and you probably shouldn't bother her. OK? I should be back in a little more than an hour. But I may be longer. Don't worry if I'm late."

Sheila nodded. She knew exactly what she and Billy would do. There was a wonderful woods at the end of their short street. It was their favorite place to play. And now when the leaves were mostly off the trees, they could have a great time playing hide and seek. Billy was fun even though he was only four—almost five.

"Bye, Mom!" Sheila and Billy waved as their mother backed out of the driveway.

"Shall we play in the woods?" Sheila asked.

"Hide and seek! Not It!" Billy yelled, and raced for the woods at the end of the street.

Sheila dutifully hid her eyes against the big oak tree in the front yard and counted.

"Ninety-nine, one hundred! Ready or not here I come!" She ran toward the woods. It was a tiny woods, though Billy called it the forest or the jungle and imagined that it was full of dragons and wizards and magicians.

The leaves rustled as she stepped off the sidewalk. She knew Billy's favorite hiding places, but she didn't want to find him right away. She walked around all the trees near the edge of the woods, knowing that he was probably hiding behind one fifty feet away on the other side or else in the hollow log they had discovered last spring, though he was getting almost too big to fit in it any more.

"I'm getting close," she called, from almost as far away as she could be and still be in the woods. She kicked the leaves and made noise. "Here I come," she warned. "No. Not there . . . Now where can he be? He must have found a new place to hide!" She talked out loud, feeling very grown up and responsible. She'd give him a lot of fun and make him think she couldn't find him.

Finally, she approached his favorite tree, still making lots of noise. She walked around it slowly, giving him time to move around to the other side, but she heard only her own footsteps rustling the leaves. She ran around the tree. No. He wasn't here. The hollow log, then. She walked over to the hollow log, expecting to see the tip of his red hat or the soles of his shoes sticking out. She knew how big he'd gotten, even if he didn't. But the hollow log was empty. He wasn't there. Hmm. He must have found a new place to hide.

Sheila stood still and thought for a minute. Where could he be? She could see almost the whole woods from where she stood. She'd really gone all around it when she started looking. Could he have hidden someplace else? Not in the woods? But she'd heard his feet crunching the leaves when he ran to hide. She hadn't heard him come out. There was a big high fence at the other side of the woods so she knew he couldn't have gone out the other side.

She walked slowly through the woods again, checking every bush and tree.

"Billy? Where are you?" She was careful not to sound scared but she was beginning to feel unsure. She left the woods and went all around the house. The house was locked up and she had the key. Billy didn't have a key. He wasn't big enough. She checked the yard next door, at Mrs. Strawn's house. He wasn't there and she was pretty sure he wasn't inside. He knew they weren't supposed to bother Mrs. Strawn.

"Billy! Billy?" No answer.

"Billy!?

"All-y all-y in free!" she yelled. No answer. No running footsteps. Now she was worried.

"Billee! Where are you? No more game, Billy. Come out, come out wherever you are!"

She stopped and listened. A wave of panic rose—she felt like throwing up. Where was he?

"Don't be scared," she told herself. "He's gotta be here somewhere. He can't have disappeared.

"Shall I ring Mrs. Strawn's bell? But I'm not supposed to bother her. I know. I'll go all through the woods, bit by bit." She looked at her watch. 4:30 already. Mother had been gone almost an hour.

She'd go through the woods methodically. If she didn't find him, she'd call Daddy—or Mother at the doctor's—or something. But she'd find him.

She started at the edge of the woods and walked all along, feeling silly but knowing that being organized was important. She turned in three steps and started back again.

"Billy! Billy!" She kept calling and listening, feeling foolish and scared. "Billy!"

She was almost halfway across the woods when her foot slipped on some leaves and she went tumbling into a hole.

She sat up and shook her head to clear it. She didn't remember a hole or a ditch. It must have been covered with leaves. She wasn't hurt but she was wet! She'd landed in a puddle at the bottom of the hole. She looked around and shuffled through the leaves. She realized the hole was deep—almost as deep as her head—and pretty big. Some leaves were hanging overhead, making a kind of cave—and then she saw it! There was a giant—well, it looked like a giant bubble, and Billy was inside! He was crying but she couldn't hear anything.

"Billy!"

He kept on crying and rubbing his eyes. He hadn't even seen her.

"*Billy!*"

He looked up and reached out. "Shi-shi!" She could see him calling but she couldn't hear him. She looked at the bubble. It looked like a giant soap bubble. She touched it. It didn't break. She found a stick in the puddle and poked the bubble, hard. It gave a little but it didn't break.

She looked at it carefully. It was clear but she could see the spectrum of the rainbow where the sun hit the bubble: orange, yellow, green, blue, violet, red. If the bubble was a soap bubble it had to break sometime. She'd learned that in her science unit on soap bubbles. If you watched carefully you could tell when a soap bubble was going to break.

Billy was scared. He was crying again. She smiled at him and tried to make him understand that she'd rescue him. She examined the bubble again, going as far around it as she could. She looked at her watch again. Quarter past five. That late! The sun would set soon. And Mother would be home. She couldn't leave Billy now. What should she do? Oh, and she had been so sure she was old enough to baby-sit.

There! She saw it! The sign. The colors in the bubble were gone. For a split second it was black.

"Billy," she called. "Billy! It's OK. The bubble's going to break!" She knew he couldn't hear her but she felt better if she kept talking to him. There was a soft but definite pllp! and suddenly there was no more bubble.

"Sheila!" Billy was sobbing and he rushed at her and they fell over in the leaves together.

She hugged him and holding his hand, they climbed out of the hole.

"What happened, Billy? How did you get in the bubble?"

"I don't know. I was hiding behind my tree and something black went over my head and someone picked me up and shoved me down the hole. When I got the thing off my head I was inside and I couldn't get out. There wasn't anyone there but this was." Billy handed her a crumpled paper towel with marks on it.

She carried it with them to the house. Mother's car was in the driveway and the light was on in the kitchen.

"There you are," Mother said as Sheila and Billy walked in. She hugged and kissed them. "Where have you been? I was just about to start looking for you.

"Why, Billy, you've been crying. What happened?"

Billy and Sheila told her.

"—and look at this," Sheila said as she flattened out the crumpled paper towel on the kitchen table. "Look. There's writing on it! In marker. It says, 'Pay $100 or you'll never see your brother again!'

"Mommy, it's like a ransom note!"

"Let me see," Mother frowned. "This is the strangest story I've ever heard. But you're all right, Billy?"

Billy sniffed and nodded.

"And you're all right, Shi-shi?"

"I'm OK. I wonder who wrote that note. Maybe I can find out."

"I think we'd better call the police." Mother moved toward the phone.

"No, wait, Mom. I think I can find out. Really."

II

Just about then, Dad walked in. "Mother's right, Sheila. This is a matter for the police." He was definite.

"But I really think I can tell who wrote the note. Then we'd know who wanted to scare us. I mean, if it was someone who really wanted to kidnap Billy, like a grown up, wouldn't they have taken him away?"

"Well, maybe you can help the police." Dad dialed the phone. "They're sending someone right over. Now you're sure you're both OK? Billy?"

Billy looked at all of them. "Ye-es. Once Shi-shi found me. I was scared but she even knew when the bubble was going to break."

Blue, white, and red lights flashed through the window.

"That was quick. They're here." Dad strode to the front door as the bell rang. "Come in!"

"Mr. O'Connor? Sergeant Blackman. What's the story?"

Once the sergeant got them to speak one at a time, it didn't take long.

"All right. Now, I have a few questions. Do you—any of you—and that includes Sheila and Billy, have any enemies?"

"Oh no. Of course not," said Mrs. O'Connor.

Dad shook his head.

Sheila looked at Billy and he looked back at her.

"Anyone in school, kids, who might have some reason to scare you, who might want to get back at you for something?"

"Oh, I'm sure not, Sergeant Blackman. Sheila has lots of friends. She's very popular and well liked. Billy goes to nursery school three days a week. I'm sure neither of them has enemies."

Billy and Sheila looked at each other again but neither of them spoke.

"Well, if you think of anything, give me a call. I'm glad both the kids are OK. I'll look over the spot now as well as I can, and we'll do a thorough investigation for clues in the daylight."

"How about the note?" Sheila asked. "Couldn't you check it for fingerprints?"

"No. You need a clean, hard surface to get good fingerprints. If I tried to get fingerprints I'd most likely find all of yours. Not much chance of getting a clear set of prints off a crumpled paper towel."

"Keep a close eye on your children, Mr. and Mrs. O'Connor, and do let us know if anything else happens or if you think of anyone who might wish to scare or harm you or the kids." Sergeant Blackman smiled at them all and closed the door behind him.

"That wasn't real helpful," Dad said, as the headlight beams disappeared.

"It certainly wasn't," his wife agreed.

"I still think I can find out who might have written the note," Sheila said.

"Sheila, that's very nice, dear, but if the police can't do it, I don't see how you can expect to. Now, let's all have supper and then, Shi-shi, you'd better get your homework done and get to bed."

Later, when Sheila went to bed, she lay awake, thinking.

"Shi-shi?"

"How come you're still awake?"

Billy padded over and got into her bed.

"Are you still scared?"

She could feel his head nod.

"Who do you think might have done it?" she asked him. She knew what she was thinking. They'd had a babysitter last summer. Betsy Rivers was fourteen. She'd been mean and they'd complained to Mommy about her. Then she didn't come any more. Sheila had seen her on the way to school and she'd threatened to get back at them.

"You're a better detective than that old policeman," Billy said. "How did you know when the bubble was going to break? How can you tell who wrote the note?"

"Well, the note was written in Magic Marker, right?"

"Yeah."

"Well, different Magic Markers are made up of different colors."

"No. It was a black marker."

"You're right. But black Magic Markers are different. If I can do an experiment, I might be able to tell what kind of marker wrote the note."

"What 'speriment?"

"You go back to your own bed, now, and we'll see about it in the morning. You're OK. You're safe and you'll see, we'll find out who did it!"

Two days later Sheila had done her experiment. In fact, she had done it on the original note and two times more on different paper towels. She'd gotten her friends in school to help her collect samples of writing in black magic marker on paper towels. By the end of the week she was pretty sure she knew who had written the note.

Use this story for lessons about

Soap bubbles
Tension
Color spectrum
Light
Sounds as clues; listening to learn
Paper chromatography

The Crystal Cabinet
after "The Glass Cupboard" by Terry Jones

Long ago there was a queen of great wisdom and caring who ruled the world.

In her palace, beside the throne, stood a crystal cabinet whose facets showed every color of the rainbow, and whose beauty all admired. This cabinet, transparent and shining, had a most astonishing quality: it produced whatever was needed.

People came to the queen and petitioned for the things they needed: seed to plant next year's crop, money to educate a child, medicine to cure the sick. If the queen agreed that the need was real, she went to the cabinet, reached in, and drew forth the item requested. There was one requirement: the petitioner must put something into the crystal cabinet in return. It didn't matter what it was, but there must be a gift of some kind for the cabinet.

The wisdom of the queen and the generosity of the cabinet were known and celebrated. Most people felt secure knowing that the cabinet was there for emergencies.

Far away from the capital city there were three thieves. They worked together to steal from everyone in a town, and when they had impoverished that town, they moved on and did the same thing to the next one.

One night as they divided the spoils of their latest victims, Scapin the schemer, complained. "We work too hard for what we get!"

"You know an easier way to be rich?" sneered Gowk.

"Yeah. I have a plan. I know a way to have whatever we want whenever we want it and no work."

"How?" demanded Gowk and Churl.

"You've heard of the crystal cabinet?"

"Of course."

"You think we're stupid? Ya gotta pay it," snorted Churl.

"Not if it's ours," replied Scapin.

"Great idea. Sure, we'll just walk in and take it! Stupid! It's guarded night and day in the great queen's throne room. We couldn't even get in to see it!"

"Ordinarily that's true. But I've heard that the queen is going to visit her sick mother. She'll be gone for some weeks. I have a plan. While she is away . . ."

The three men traveled to the capital city. They listened and learned all they could about the palace, the guards, and the queen's plans. Very late one moonless night when only one young guard was on duty, they crept into the palace and overpowered him.

"Is that it?" asked Gowk.

"Yeah. Beautiful isn't it?" Scapin stared. The three men were awed. "And it's ours. All we have to do is get it outta here. You two are the strongest. You carry it and I'll go ahead and make sure the way is clear."

"I don't need him to help me. I'll carry it myself," said Churl. "Just help me get it on my back."

But lifting the cabinet was not so easy. It was fragile but it was far heavier than any of them imagined. Sweating and cursing, the three thieves hauled the cabinet from the throne room, down corridors and stairways.

"Don't let it slip!"

"Steady, you goon!"

"Stairs here. Don't let it crash!"

"Damn you! I know what I'm doing. Why don't you help, you weakling!"

At last, deep in the forest, they set it down.

"Now we got it, thanks to me!" Scapin rubbed his hands eagerly. "I'll help myself first!"

"You'd never have gotten it here without us," said Churl, "and don't you forget it! Why you're too weak to even budge it!"

"Shut up! I want a bag of gold!" and Scapin stuck his hand into the cabinet. The bag of gold was so heavy he had trouble lifting it out of the cabinet.

"We go shares!" cried Gowk.

"Get your own!"

Each of the others demanded a bag of gold and pulled it from the cabinet. They sat with their bags and counted the gold piece by piece. They were all the same.

"I'm tired. I'm going to get some sleep," said Scapin. The others agreed and soon they were all asleep and snoring, their heads on their coveted bags of gold.

In the middle of the night, Scapin stirred. "Good. They're sleeping. I'll just help myself to more. I deserve more. If it hadn't been for me, we wouldn't have the thing at all." And he pulled one—no, three more bags from the cabinet. He hid them under his coat and went back to sleep.

Well, you know what happened. The others woke in turn and took gold from the cabinet until by morning, each had a veritable mountain of riches.

"Diamonds!" sneered Scapin as he reached into the cabinet.

"Platinum!" cried Churl. He staggered under the weight of the bars of precious metal.

"Look out, you clumsy oaf!" shouted Scapin as Churl tripped and fell into Scapin's pile.

"Watch out yourself!" cried Churl and he began to hurl Scapin's treasure onto his own pile.

Bags of riches were snatched from one pile and thrown onto another. Gowk threw a great bag of jewels at Scapin. Scapin fell back, nursing a black eye and bloody nose. He threw a bag of something at Gowk and then another at Churl. One by one, they fell, bleeding, furious, injured. One flying bag missed its mark and crashed into the crystal cabinet, shattering it into thousands of pieces.

There was a moment's stunned silence and then the three men roared and swung at one another. After a while, all was still and only the vultures circled, waiting.

When the courtiers discovered the cabinet missing, they were in despair.

"What shall we do?"

"Send for the queen. She will tell us . . ."

"No. She will be angry. Let's find the cabinet ourselves. That way we never need to tell her what happened."

"She'll know."

David, a young page, listened. "I'll go and find it while they're still arguing." He crept from the throne room.

When the queen returned from her visit, she asked what had happened to the crystal cabinet and the story poured forth.

"Go," she said sadly. "Search where you can, to the furthest reaches of the planet."

As they set forth David slipped into the throne room.

"What is it, my boy?" The queen leaned forward.

David opened his handkerchief. In it lay thousands of glistening shards of crystal. He told the queen how he went searching and flashes of light caught his eye and guided him to the piles of treasure, the three rotting corpses, and the shattered remains of the crystal cabinet.

"I picked up all the pieces I could find and brought them home."

"You have done well, my boy," said the queen. She sent for her master glassmakers.

"Your Majesty," they told her, "we cannot make another crystal cabinet, but we can melt the shards in our furnace and recast the glass in some other form."

"Do the best you can," she told them.

They melted down the precious shards of crystal and cast them into a beautiful blue-green globe that hangs, to this day, in the throne room of the queen of wisdom and caring. It does not give gifts to petitioners. The requests of those whose petitions seem reasonable to the queen are sometimes partly filled from the reclaimed stolen treasure.

David grew up to be the special guardian of the globe, a storyteller who told wonderful tales of days of old, when the crystal cabinet had bountiful plenty for all who put something back into the cabinet to pay for and replenish what they had received. The beautiful blue-green globe that hangs there still reminds us all that we need to replenish the earth.

Use this story for lessons about

> Ecology
> Renewable resources
> Crystals
> Glass blowing/manufacturing/properties

It was a fine day. Nasradin was going to the mill to have his wheat ground into flour. He loaded his donkey with great bags of wheat. One after another, his neighbors looked out and saw Nasradin busy about his task.

"Nasradin," Achmed asked, "Are you taking your wheat to the mill?"

"I am," Nasradin replied.

"If I load up my donkey, will you drive her along too?"

"Of course."

"And mine?" asked Erhan.

"And mine?"

Soon, Nasradin had his own donkey and nine of his neighbors' donkeys, all loaded with wheat for the mill. He climbed up on his donkey and set off. Keeping the donkeys on the path was tricky. They wanted to wander here and there, to eat the delicious wild flowers of late summer. Nasradin had his hands full.

After a while, he thought it best to count the donkeys to make sure he hadn't lost any. That would be awful.

He sat on his donkey and counted: "One, two, three, four, five, six, seven, eight, nine. Only nine donkeys? There should be ten. This is terrible. Maybe I missed one."

He counted again. "One, two, three, four, five, six, seven, eight, nine." Where had he lost that tenth donkey?

"I'll get off my donkey and count again," he thought. "One, two, three, four, five, six, seven, eight, nine, ten!" What a relief! They were all there!

He climbed back on his donkey and started off again. The day was warm. The sun shone. Nasradin had done all that work loading his donkey. He had waited patiently while his neighbors loaded their donkeys. The pleasant rocking motion of the donkey's slow pace was soothing. Nasradin's head nodded. He slept.

The donkey stumbled on a rock and then recovered her footing. Nasradin awoke. He looked wildly around. He remembered where he was: taking his wheat—oh, and his neighbors' wheat—to the mill. Were all the donkeys still there? He had better count.

"One, two, three, four, five, six, seven, eight, nine—Only nine? There were supposed to be ten. Where was the tenth donkey?"

He counted again. Nine donkeys. And again. Only nine. He got off his own donkey and counted one more time. "One, two, three, four, five, six, seven, eight, nine, ten!" They were all there!

"I had better walk," said Nasradin to himself. "There always seem to be ten donkeys when I walk. That way I'll be sure!"

Use this story for lessons about:

Counting 1–10
Counting yourself

Once there was an old woman who lived alone and who loved to make rice cakes. Every morning she made nice round rice cakes. One sunny morning, a rice cake rolled away from her.

"Come back, little rice cake," she called. But the rice cake kept right on rolling. It rolled all the way across the table. The old woman ran around the table to catch the rice cake. But the rice cake was fast. It fell from the table. She tried to catch it, to scoop it up from the dirt floor, but the floor opened up and the rice cake disappeared down a hole.

"Come back, little rice cake!" she called.

But the rice cake was gone. Suddenly the hole got larger and the little old woman found herself tumbling over and over down a long steep hill and when she got to the bottom and stopped, she found herself in a strange underground world. There was a road that went here and there. All along the road were statues of gods.

"Come back, little rice cake!" the little old woman called. She began to run along the road as fast as she could.

"Come back, little rice cake!" She panted. She came to a statue of a god. "Have you seen my rice cake?" she asked.

The statue spoke. "Your rice cake rolled past here ten minutes ago. Do not follow your rice cake. There are dangerous monsters at the end of the road!"

"I'm not afraid of monsters! I want my rice cake!" said the little old woman and she ran on, faster than ever.

"Come back, little rice cake!" she called. Soon she came to a second statue of a god. "Good morning," she panted, remembering her manners. "Have you seen my rice cake?"

"Good morning, Little Old Woman. I saw your rice cake five minutes ago, but please do not follow your rice cake. Dangerous monsters live at the end of the road."

"I am not afraid of monsters. I want my rice cake!" cried the little old woman and she ran on twice as fast as before.

"Come back, little rice cake! Come back!" she panted. She came to a third god. "Oh please, have you seen my rice cake?" she asked, panting, for she was all worn out.

"It just went by here but—quick! Hide behind me! Here comes a monster!"

The little old woman hid behind the statue.

"Good morning," said the god to the monster who was indeed a terrifying sight.

"Good morn—" growled the monster. He stopped and sniffed the air. "I smell a human being!"

"Oh no. I'm sure it's just the smell of the river," replied the god. "I don't thi—"

At that moment, the little old woman sneezed.

"Ah ha!" growled the monster and he reached his long, hairy hand behind the statue and grabbed the little old woman.

"Aaaiyee!" she shrieked, for the monster was, indeed, a terrifying sight.

The monster looked at her. He shifted his huge hand so it was around her waist and turned back to the river.

"Please don't hurt the little old woman," the statue begged. "She was only looking for her rice cake!"

"I'll take her home and she can make rice cakes for us. Monsters love rice cakes!" He turned around and walked back down to the river, carrying the little old woman.

He put her in a row boat and took up the oars. He rowed and rowed across the wide river. Soon a strange looking house came in sight on the opposite bank of the river. It was enormous. It loomed over the river. When the boat touched the shore, the monster picked up the little old woman and carried her into the strange house. He set her down in the kitchen and handed her a wooden paddle.

"You will cook rice for us," he growled. "Listen to how you do it!"

The little old woman was sure she knew all about cooking rice and had since long before the monster was born. But he looked scary and very, very big, so she listened.

"Put just one grain of rice in the pot. Stir it with the paddle. It will become a whole pot of rice."

The little old woman listened. She was too scared to speak so she nodded. The monster turned on his heels and left the kitchen.

The little old woman looked around. There was plenty of rice— bags and bags of it. Why bother with just one grain? But then she thought she had better do as the monster said. She took just one grain of rice and put it in the pot. She took the special wooden paddle and began to stir the grain of rice in the pot.

"Look!" The one became two, the two four, the four eight, the eight sixteen, the sixteen thirty-two, the thirty-two sixty-four, the sixty-four a hundred and twenty-eight, the hundred and twenty-eight two hundred and fifty-six and the pot was full! It was kind of fun! It was like magic! She made the rice into rice cakes. She made more rice and more rice cakes. She made rice and rice cakes by the hour, by the day, by the week. All day long she made delicious rice cakes and the monsters ate them all up. (They just loved rice cakes!)

One day the little old woman was tired of the monsters just eating and eating and eating her delicious rice cakes. There was no end to their appetites and besides, she wanted to be in her own home, making her own rice cakes.

She looked. No monsters in sight. She stuck the magic paddle in the sash of her kimono. She tiptoed out of the house and down to the river. She looked to the left—no monsters! She looked to the right—no monsters! And the boat was there!

She stepped into the boat and began to row. She rowed and rowed and when she was in the middle of the river she looked up! There, staring at her from their bank of the river was a throng of horrible looking monsters! They grinned at her. She began to shake!

The monsters couldn't swim but they all leaned over and began to suck up all the water in the river. It slurped and gurgled into their mouths with a disgusting noise! The water in the river went down, down, down. The boat bumped on the mud bottom of the river. The little old woman jumped out of the boat and tried to run across the mud. Her feet stuck in the mud! When she tried to pull them out, she fell over on her head and her head was stuck in the mud.

The monsters had never seen such a funny sight! They started to laugh!

"Ho-ho-ho-ho ha-ha-ha-ha!" But they couldn't laugh and keep the river in their mouths. The water flooded back into the river and the little old woman got unstuck and climbed back into the boat!

She rowed and rowed and rowed until the boat bumped on the opposite bank of the river, and then she jumped out of the boat and ran back up the road to her house.

She took a pot from her shelf and set it on her stove. She put one grain of rice—only one—in the pot and she began to stir.

"Look!" The one became two, the two four, the four eight, the eight sixteen, the sixteen thirty-two, the thirty-two sixty-four, the sixty-four a hundred and twenty-eight, the hundred and twenty-eight two hundred and fifty-six and the pot was full! It was kind of fun! It was like magic!

She looked around her house. It all looked the same. Oh, a few cobwebs here and there, for she had been gone a long time. She settled herself down and made rice cakes. Delicious rice cakes, and as far as I know, she is making them still!

Use this story for lessons about:

> Doubling numbers (powers of two)
> Multiplication
> Volume
> Absorption of liquid
> Speed/distance
> Energy

Rosie and David
by Barbara Lipke

"Come on, Dave, we want to get going while the tide's slack."

"I'm coming. I've got the bait. The lines are on the boat. You got lunch?"

"Of course. Mom said to watch the weather." David joined in with "Watch the weather." That's what Rosie's mom always said.

"When I picked up the bait at the shack they said the blues were running," David said.

"I hope we don't catch any. I'm tired of bluefish and the store hardly pays for 'em. They'll only take them if they're cleaned and scaled and all. Maybe we'll catch stripers."

"You wish!"

"What I wish is that there was enough money for Mom to get new tires for the car. She said she needed four hundred dollars for tires. She almost got fired yesterday because she had a flat and the spare was no good. Her boss was mad because she was late again." David listened sympathetically. Rosie's mom had a hard time.

They clambered aboard the old whaler and pushed off the jetty. David turned the key in the outboard. It coughed twice. They drifted in the slack tide. He tried it again and this time it caught. They had permission to use the boat on calm days as long as they stayed close to shore. They'd been fishing together since they were real little. Now Rosie was ten and David almost ten.

As soon as they were clear of the jetty and into the bay David headed the boat to their favorite fishing spot. It wasn't too far off shore and when the tide came in a little they could beach the boat and eat lunch in their secret cave. Rosie caught a sea cucumber.

"Ugh! Disgusting thing. Why'd it have to snag my bait?" She cut it free and threw it back into the water.

"Hey, at least you caught something."

After a while David got a bite and pulled up a tinker mackerel. "Better than nothing," he said. He put it, still flopping, in the white plastic bucket.

"Fog," Rosie observed. It was coming in, and coming in fast. Within a minute or two everything was white and damp and they could no longer see the shore.

David cut the motor. "The tide's on the way in," he explained. "I don't know where we are, exactly, but the tide will carry us toward the shore. Let's eat while we wait for this to lift."

They opened their lunch bag and unwrapped peanut butter and jelly sandwiches.

"Did you bring water?"

Rosie pulled out the juice bottle of water and they each took a swallow.

"What's that?"

"What?" Rosie looked where he was looking. There was a dark lump in the water a couple of yards off their bow. "I don't know." She scrambled to the bow of the whaler and looked at the lump floating nearby. "I'll pull it in with the boat hook." She reached down for the boat hook and pulled and prodded the dark shape close to the boat. "Looks like a garbage bag." She grabbed the bag with one hand. It was wet and slimy. There was seaweed clinging to it. She tried to lift it into the boat.

"Ugh. Weighs a ton. Give me a hand, Dave."

Together they pulled the heavy bag aboard.

"What could be in it?" Rosie looked at David.

"Garbage?"

"A body?" Rosie shivered.

"Not heavy enough. A treasure?"

"You wish!"

"There's only one way to find out. Let's open it."

"Go ahead," Rosie said, staring at the bag as though it might contain something alive.

David untied the knot in the top of the bag. It was one of those double ones and only tore a little. The two heads came together over the open mouth of the bag. Another bag was inside, even more tightly knotted, and it sat in a pool of sea water. Rosie tried to undo the knot. David got a screwdriver from the tackle box. They pried the knot apart and looked inside. Another bag!

"This is silly," Rosie exclaimed.

"No. Whoever tied these up, wanted to be sure that what was inside stayed dry. This bag looks totally dry."

Inside the third black and brown bag were six packages, brick shaped, solid and heavy, each tightly wrapped in tape-sealed white plastic wastebasket bags.

The two children looked at each other. David cut the tape on one of the bags.

"It's money! Real money! Look at that—they're twenty dollar bills! I've never seen so much money."

They began to count the bills.

"A hundred. Twenty, forty, sixty, eighty, two hundred."

"How much, do you think?"

The boat bumped gently on sand.

"The tide carried us in. Where are we?" The two children tried to peer through the fog. It was thicker. They could see only a few feet of beach. They jumped over the side and pulled the boat up until it was totally out of the water. Rosie carried the anchor further up the beach and dropped it behind a rock. She pushed the anchor fluke into the sand and under the rock with her foot.

She shivered. "I'm cold."

"Hey look, Rosie, here's our cave. We're right where we wanted to be! Let's take the bag and count the money." They drained the water from the two outer bags and carried their find into the cave.

The cave was barely an indent in the low cliffs with a hollow place behind one side. It was just big enough for the two children to sit, out of sight of anyone passing on the beach. At high tide the water came up to the entrance. Today the cave was wholly cut off from sight. The boat disappeared in the fog.

"How many bills are there in this package?" Rosie sat cross-legged with the brick of money in her lap.

"A hundred?" David guessed. "Let's see. That would be two hundred dollars—no, two thousand."

"I think there's more than a hundred. It'll take too long to count it all. Let's estimate. Look, here's ten. That's barely even an eighth of an inch. This must be about two inches thick. Let's try the thumb measure." They measured the thickness of the block of bills by the first thumb joint.

"Almost two inches. Suppose there are five hundred twenty dollar bills. How much is that?"

Rosie drew the figures in the sand and multiplied. "Ten thousand dollars? Ten thousand dollars! What are we going to do with it?"

"Is it real? I mean, it could be counterfeit!"

"But the bills aren't new. Wouldn't counterfeit money be like new bills?"

"I don't know. It's scary. How did the money get in the bags and in the water?"

"Somebody did it. Why? Where's it come from?" They sat and thought. "It must have been in the water a while. There's all that seaweed and stuff on the outside bag," Rosie said.

"Are the other packages the same?"

They opened another white plastic wrapped brick. There was another stack of bills held together with rubber bands.

"This one's ten dollar bills." She looked through the stack. "No. There are some fives and some twenties here."

They opened other packages and riffled through the bills. The third one seemed to be all twenties. The fourth one was mixed again. David thought he saw a couple of fifties and a hundred dollar bill. There were still two unopened packages.

"What should we do?" Rosie asked.

"It's too much to keep. It might be fifty thousand dollars. It's a lot of money. I guess we should tell our parents and maybe the police."

"Do you think anyone knows how much? I mean, would it matter if we kept enough to buy tires for Mom's car? Who would know?"

They counted out four hundred dollars. Rosie stuck it in her jeans' pocket.

"Are you going to take any?"

David shook his head. "It feels funny."

They wrapped up the money in its packages and retied each of the three plastic bags.

The fog was thicker than ever when they ventured from the cave. The tide had come further in and the boat floated gently. Rosie tested the anchor rope. The anchor was firm. They knew the way home by land, over the path and the road, even in the fog. They knew they shouldn't try to go by boat. Too much chance of getting really lost.

They left the bag in Rosie's cellar and went to see Bert the Tire Man. He was not their favorite person. He was big and he looked scary. They paid for four tires and Bert promised to mount them on Rosie's mom's car. He looked at them suspiciously.

"Where'd you kids get this money?"

"My uncle sent it to me and asked me to get the tires for Mom's birthday for a surprise." Rosie was surprised at how easily the lie slipped off her tongue.

"Yeah?" he growled. "You two been fishing?"

They nodded.

"In this fog?" he growled again and leered at them. "Catch anything?"

David gulped. "A sea cucumber and a tinker mackerel. Then it got too foggy to stay out."

They went back to Rosie's house. Neither of their parents were home. They took the garbage bag and went to the police station.

"Hi, kids, been fishing? What'd you catch?" The police chief, John Donalson, loved to tease them.

"Money," David said.

"Yeah? Want to share your secret fishing hole?"

Rosie set the garbage bag down on the floor and opened it. David opened the two inside bags and the chief peered in. He pulled out a white package and looked. He whistled.

"Better tell me about this," he said.

They told him the whole story.

"Let's go back to your boat and I'll take a closer look. There's a lot of money here. Do you know how much?"

They shook their heads. "Maybe forty-fifty thousand dollars?" Rosie guessed.

The chief locked the gabage bag in the police safe.

"Whose is it, do you think?" David asked as they got into the police car for the ride back.

"I haven't any idea. Nobody has reported it missing so I think it's probably not honest money."

"What do you mean?"

"Well, if you had that much money, would you carry it around in garbage bags and maybe toss it overboard into the bay?"

"I'd put it in the bank," said Rosie.

"So it's drug dealers or bank robbers?" David sounded excited.

"What happens to it then?" Rosie asked.

"Well, we have to hold onto it. It's evidence. If there are no legal claims on it after a year, I guess it'll belong to you two—probably in trust to your parents until you're old enough to have it yourselves." He parked the car at the end of the grassy lane. The fog had lifted and they could see their boat, tugging at the anchor rope, afloat in shallow water.

"Hold it," said Chief Donalson, as Rosie and David started to run to the boat. "Not so fast. Were there footprints here before?"

David and Rosie stopped short and looked at each other and then at the damp sand. There were big footprints leading to the water's edge, near the boat.

"I don't think so," David began.

"It was so foggy we didn't see anything—but, David, we had to look down in order to find the path in the fog. There weren't any footprints."

"Yeah. You're right. And whoever those prints belong to went straight for our boat."

"All right, kids. Sh!" Chief Donalson put his forefinger to his lips and motioned them silently back the way they had come.

When they were back in the car, he backed away as quietly as he could and started back toward town.

"But . . ." Rosie started to protest.

"Whoever is looking for that money didn't leave the boat," the chief explained. "The footprints only go one way, *toward* the boat. He's looking for his money and *you*. Are your parents home?"

Rosie shook her head. "Mom's at work."

"And my mother and dad are downtown shopping. Mrs. Cranston's is where we're supposed to go if we need anything."

The chief thought. "I'm going to need help and you two need to be safe."

"What do you mean, safe? Why can't we just go home and hang around the house?"

"I think whoever lost that money is looking for it, and maybe for you. He could be dangerous!"

The chief made some telephone calls. "I don't want to lock the two of you up," he explained to Rosie and David, "but you stay right here in the police station. No going out, understand?"

They nodded and watched him drive away with the two other police officers in another car.

"How did Footprints know where to look for us and who we were?" Rosie asked.

"He might have seen us fish the bag out of the water."

"It was too foggy. Besides, if he had, wouldn't he have taken it back then? Or when we were in the cave?"

"How else could he have known?"

They were quiet, thinking.

"The tires!" David said, suddenly.

"The tires? What do you mean?"

"Remember Bert the Tire Man asked where we got the money? We didn't have the bag with us, but he asked if we'd been fishing. We had stashed the garbage bag in your basement!"

"He must have thought we left it on the boat!"

"Do you think Bert is Footprints?"

"He could be. His feet are big enough."

"If the footprints match, that'll prove he's the one!"

"But the tide! It'll wash out the footprints! We have to get to the police! Maybe they can measure the footprints or something!"

"We promised to stay here!"

"But—"

"It's OK, kids," Chief Donalson said, as he came back into the station. "We thought about that. We have a plaster cast of the footprints and we think we've got our man! We also found some fingerprints on the boat.

"Now I have to ask you if you took any of the money?"

Rosie nodded and hung her head. "I wanted to get new tires for Mom's car. She almost lost her job because she couldn't get to work. I took four hundred dollars and bought tires from Bert. I told him my uncle sent it so I could buy Mom a birthday present. He must have figured we found the money."

"You do know you shouldn't have taken the money, don't you?"

Rosie nodded, her head still down.

"We've been watching Bert for a long time. His business is a perfect cover for buying and selling drugs. We think we have him now. I guess we could call the four hundred dollars your reward for catching the criminal!"

Use this story for lessons about:

Estimation
Counting
Money
Weight
Tides
Fog
Perception
Moral issue: Should Rosie have taken the $400?

Tailor

Traditional

Once there was a tailor. He was a hard-working man who made clothes for all the men in the village. He worked all day every day and sometimes into the evening by candlelight. He had one wish. He knew just what he wanted. He wanted to make himself a coat. He had seen the material he wanted when he was in town buying supplies: it was the shade of blue the sky is between sunset and dark, and it had just a glint of silver here and there throughout the cloth.

Each evening he counted out the pennies he had earned and he put one or two aside, in a special box, to buy the material. At last he had saved enough. On his next trip to town he bought the cloth and carried it home. That night, after he had finished work, he took out the cloth and looked at it. Oh, it was beautiful! Just the color of the sky between sunset and dark, and just a glint of silver here and there throughout the cloth.

He laid out the material on his work table and carefully cut out a coat. Each night, after he finished working on the clothes he was making for the men of the village, he worked on his own coat. He stitched it and fitted it. At last it was finished. He put it on and looked at himself in the mirror he kept for his customers. Oh! It was handsome! Just what he had hoped. Look, it was just the color of the sky between sunset and dark—and here and there, a glint of silver thread throughout the coat. And it fit perfectly!

The next evening, he went for a walk in the village. Everyone admired his coat.

"Tailor, what a beautiful coat! The color is perfect—oh and look, there's just a glint of silver here and there. And the fit! Turn around, Tailor, and let me see the back!"

He wore the coat every day. He wore it all through the fall and winter and spring until at last it was too warm to wear it any longer. Then he aired it and brushed it carefully and packed it away until the weather was cool enough to take it out again.

He wore the coat for a good many years, and then, one year, as he was putting it away, he realized that it was shabby. The elbows and the cuffs and the button holes were worn. He laid the coat out on his counter and he cut away all the shabby bits. Ah, there was just enough good cloth left to make a jacket.

The jacket was beautiful. The cloth was still the color of the sky between sunset and dark. The silver thread glinted here and there. And the jacket was even more useful than the coat. He could wear it earlier in the fall and later in the spring. He could wear it on cool summer evenings and on cold winter days, he could wear it indoors as he worked.

And then, one year, he discovered that the jacket was shabby. He laid it out on his counter and he cut away all the shabby pieces—and there was just enough good cloth left to make a vest! He cut and stitched and put a row of handsome buttons down the front and he had a new vest. It was beautiful. It was the color of the sky between sunset and dark, with just a glint of silver here and there. It was even more useful than the jacket. He wore it all the time. Everyone admired it. It fit so perfectly, and the colors—mmm—beautiful!

But in time, the vest too became shabby. The tailor laid out the vest and cut away all the shabby pieces. Ah, there was just enough cloth left to make a cap. The cap was perfect. When he looked up, he could just see the edge of the bill, a perfect blue, the color of the sky between sunset and dark, and look, just a glint of silver in the cloth. At night the cap hung on the chair beside his bed and he could see the silver glint in the moonlight that shone through his window. He wore the cap night and day, indoors and out, and in time, it too became shabby.

He laid out the cap on his bench and cut away all the shabby pieces. There was just enough good cloth left to cover a button. He sewed the button on his new vest and used it to keep his needles and pins as he worked. It reminded him of the coat and the jacket and the vest and the cap. It was just the color of the sky between sunset and dark, with just a glint of silver here and there.

At last, even the button got shabby. He laid it out on his bench and cut away all the shabby pieces, and there was just enough left to make this story!

Use this story for lessons about:

> Recycling
> Measurement
> Area
> Creative thinking
> Invention and innovation
> Transformations

Appendix B
Resources

Storytelling Resources for Teachers

Baker, Augusta, and Ellen Greene. 1977. *Storytelling: Art and Technique*. New York: Bowker. A librarian's approach to storytelling. Library and child-oriented with index and bibilography.

Dailey, Sheila, ed. 1994. *Tales as Tools: The Power of Story in the Classroom*. Jonesborough, TN. National Storytelling Press. A collection of articles by storytellers and educators about their experiences working in classrooms. The book includes curriculum applications. The bibliography includes works about storytelling and grade-appropriate stories.

Gillard, Marni. 1995. *Storyteller, Storyteacher*. York, ME: Stenhouse. A teacher-teller shares her discoveries in the world of storytelling and education.

Hamilton, Martha, and Mitch Weiss. 1990. *Children Tell Stories: A Teaching Guide*. New York: Richard Owen. Written by two experienced storytellers who work in the classroom. Includes ways to teach storytelling, help children, plan storytelling events. Twenty-five stories for children to tell. Bibliography and index.

Heins, Ethel L., et al. 1983. "Storytelling Issue." *Horn Book Magazine* 59. Eight articles on various aspects of storytelling.

League for the Advancement of New England Storytelling (LANES). 1995. *New England Directory of Storytelling*. Cambridge, MA:

Yellow Moon Press. Regional guide to storytellers, concerts, festivals, and tips on producing successful storytelling events.

Livo, Norma J., and Sandra A. Reitz. 1987. *Storytelling Activities.* Littleton, CO: Libraries Unlimited. Many activities that involve the audience in storytelling and performance. Bibliography.

———. 1986. *Storytelling Process and Practice.* Littleton, CO: Libraries Unlimited. A definitive work on the history of storytelling. How to tell stories. Index, appendices, sources.

———. 1991. *Storytelling Folklore Source Book.* Englewood, NJ: Libraries Unlimited. How to explore folklore; weaving fragments into story; folk elements of stories, motifs, humor. A rich resource book.

Maguire, Jack. 1985. *Creative Storytelling.* New York: McGraw Hill. Another approach to telling stories, includes types of stories and how to modify them to fit your audience.

Miller, Teresa, Anne Pellowski, and Norma Livo, eds. 1988. *Joining In.* Cambridge, MA: Yellow Moon Press. A collection of eighteen stories for audience participation and how to tell them. Selected by storytellers.

National Storytelling Association. 1996. *National Storytelling Directory.* Jonesborough, TN: National Storytelling Press. A storytelling guide and national listing of storytellers, organizations, events, educational opportunities, periodicals, broadcast programming, and production companies. The book includes a brief storytelling guide featuring articles about community and family uses of storytelling.

Sawyer, Ruth. 1976. *The Way of the Storyteller.* New York: Penguin. An early work on why and how to tell stories.

Schimmel, Nancy. 1978. *Just Enough to Make a Story: A Sourcebook for Storytelling.* Berkeley: Sisters' Choice. Easy to use, comfortable. A good beginning guide to storytelling. Includes stories and activities.

Spolin, Viola. 1963. *Improvisation for the Theatre.* Evanston, IL: Northwestern University Press. A source for storytelling exercises.

Trousdale, Ann M., Sue A. Woestehoff, and Marni Schwartz, eds. 1994. *Give a Listen: Stories of Storytelling in School.* Urbana, IL: National Council of Teachers of English. Seventeen essays by teachers and storytellers about their experiences with storytelling, kindergarten through graduate education. Three sections: In the Beginning: How Storytellers Get Started; Making Connections: Discovering the Power of Storytelling in the Classroom; and Coming Together: Building a Community of Listeners and Learners. The book includes an annotated bibliography of resources for storytellers.

van Allsburg, Chris. 1984. *The Mysteries of Harris Burdick*. Boston: Houghton Mifflin. Pictures and captions are imaginative idea starters.

Zimmerman, Jack, and Virginia Coyle. 1991. "Council: Reviving the Art of Listening." *Utne Reader* March/April: 79–85. History and rationale for the Native American talking stick.

Science and Math Resources for Teachers

Flatow, Ira. 1989. *Rainbows, Curve Balls and Other Wonders of the Natural World Explained*. New York: Harper and Row. Brief, easy-to-understand essays explaining all sorts of natural (and man-made) phenomena.

Lipke, Barbara, and Peter N. Lipke. 1992. "Tales from Science." *Science Scope* 16 (3): 28–32.

Pappas, Theoni. 1989. *The Joy of Mathematics: Discovering Mathematics All Around You*. San Carlos, CA: Wide World Publishing/Tetra. An eclectic collection of math history and biography, puzzles, mazes, and other phenomena. Rich resource. Easy to use.

———. 1991. *More Joy of Mathematics: Exploring Mathematics All Around You*. San Carlos, CA: Wide World Publishing/Tetra. More history, puzzles, and ideas. Intriguing.

Roach, Linda E. 1992. *I Have a Story About That: Historical Vignettes to Enhance the Teaching of the Nature of Science*. Natchitoches, LA: Roach Publishing Co. Vignettes are arranged chronologically and cross referenced to scientific attitudes and disciplines. References.

Socia, Deb. 1994. "Making Math User Friendly." *Storytelling Magazine* 6 (1): 26–27.

Watson, James D. 1968. *The Double Helix*. New York: Signet Books. Readable and exciting. The Nobel laureate's story of the race to discover the shape and nature of hereditary matter.

Whitin, David J., and Sandra Wilde. 1992. *Read Any Good Math Lately? Children's Books for Mathematical Learning , K–6*. Portsmouth, NH: Heinemann. Using children's literature to teach math. Sections and extensive bibliography arranged by math discipline.

———. 1995. *It's the Story That Counts: More Children's Books for Mathematical Learning.* Portsmouth, NH: Heinemann. Lots more.

Ontario Science Centre. 1987. *Foodworks.* Reading, MA: Addison-Wesley. Stories and experiments related to the things we eat.

Stories Related to Science in Nature

Burgess, Thornton W. 1990. *Animal Tales.* New York: Platt and Munk, Putnam. Old-fashioned moral tales about animals. Sentimental, but good natural information.

———. 1952. *Adventures of Billy Mink.* New York: Grosset and Dunlap.

———. 1943. *Adventures of Chatterer.* New York: Grosset and Dunlap. Somewhat old-fashioned moral tales of animals and their habits and habitats for young children. Burgess has written many "Adventures of" stories.

Burnford, Sheila. 1961. *Incredible Journey.* Boston: Little, Brown. The exciting story of two dogs and a cat finding their way home over hundreds of miles of Canadian wilderness. Lots of good natural science.

George, Jean Craighead. 1959. *My Side of the Mountain.* New York: Dutton. A young boy from the city survives a year on his own, living in a hollow tree and making friends with animals. Exciting and full of nature lore.

———. 1968. *Coyote in Manhattan.* New York: Crowell. A girl befriends a coyote and finds self-confidence.

———. 1972. *Julie of the Wolves.* New York: Harper and Row. An Eskimo girl is raised by wolves. Exciting, a classic.

———. 1975. *Hook a Fish, Catch a Mountain.* New York: E. P. Dutton. A city girl from a family of competitive male fishermen follows the clues and finds out what happened to the "big one"!

———. 1976. *Going to the Sun.* New York: Harper and Row. Mountain goats, their habits, habitats, and survival in an exciting story.

———. 1983. *The Talking Earth.* New York: Harper and Row. Set in the Florida Everglades, this tale of a Seminole girl's coming of age in a hurricane is exciting and packed with natural science information.

George has written many other well-researched books on natural science themes.

Holling, Holling Clancy. 1941. *Paddle-to-the-Sea*. Boston: Houghton Mifflin. A young Native American boy paddles from Lake Nipigon through the Great Lakes and down the St. Lawrence River to the sea. Geography, travel, nature, ecology.

Lorenz, Konrad. 1952. *King Solomon's Ring*. New York: Time-Life. Essays on animal observation from damsel flies to ducks by a great observer of animal behavior. Content is often humorous and rich with storytelling opportunities.

Maxwell, Gavin. 1960. *Ring of Bright Water*. New York: Dutton. A naturalist observes the life cycle of the otters he studies and befriends. Beautifully written, touching.

Mowat, Farley. 1961. *Owls in the Family*. Boston: Little, Brown. A boy adopts owls. Humorous. Good natural facts. All ages.

———. 1963. *Never Cry Wolf*. Boston: Little, Brown. A naturalist, sent to find information on "killer wolves," learns what they are really like. Humorous, touching.

North, Sterling. 1963. *Rascal*. London: Puffin. A year in the lives of a boy and a raccoon. Hilarious, accurate.

———. 1965. *Little Rascal*. New York: Dutton. More fun with raccoons.

———. 1966. *Raccoons Are the Brightest People*. New York: Dutton.

Seton, Ernest Thompson. 1926. *Wild Animals I Have Known*. New York: Scribner. Sentimental stories of wild animals.

White, E. B. 1952. *Charlotte's Web*. New York: Harper and Row. Charlotte the spider teaches Fern about life in this children's classic.

Stories Related to Ecology

Brody, Ed, et al. 1992. *Spinning Tales, Weaving Hope: Stories of Peace, Justice and the Environment*. Philadelphia: New Society. Thirty-two stories, chosen by storytellers, with follow-up activities to use in classrooms and with other groups.

Burnford, Sheila. 1973. *Mr. Noah and the Second Flood*. New York: Praeger. Moral tale, set in the future, about what to rescue in the second great flood.

Cherry, Lynne. 1990. *The Great Kapock Tree*. New York: Harcourt Brace Jovanovich. A beautifully illustrated story about the far-reaching effects of cutting down one tree in the Amazon rain forest.

George, Jean Craighead. 1975. *Hook a Fish, Catch a Mountain*. New York: E.P. Dutton. See *Stories Related to Science in Nature*.

Jones, Terry. 1983. "The Glass Cupboard." In *Fairy Tales*. New York: Penguin. The original story that became "The Crystal Cabinet."

van Allsburg, Chris. 1990. *Just a Dream*. Boston: Houghton Mifflin. A boy dreams about the future after the earth has been destroyed through carelessness.

Zolotow, Charlotte. 1962. *When the Wind Stops*. London: Abelard-Schuman. What happens when the wind stops. Good information. Young children.

Legends and Myths

Clark, Ella E. 1966. *Indian Legends from the Northern Rockies*. Norman: University of Oklahoma Press. An ethnographic collection that includes many "pourquoi" stories.

Green, Roger Lancelyn. 1970. *Tales of Ancient Egypt*. Harmondsworth, England: Puffin. Ancient beliefs portrayed in fascinating tales.

Hamilton, Edith. 1953. *Greek Mythology*. New York: Dutton. Classic retelling of Greek myths.

Hamilton, Virginia. 1988. *In the Beginning: Creation Stories from Around the World*. New York: Harcourt Brace Jovanovich. A collection of creation myths from many cultures.

Melzack, Ronald. 1970. *Raven, Creator of the World*. Toronto: McClelland and Stewart. Raven is the Inuit creator and trickster who sometimes does the right thing.

Reid, Bill, and Robert Bringhurst. 1984. *The Raven Steals the Light*. Vancouver: Douglas and McIntyre. More tales of Raven, some earthy.

Thomson, David. 1989. *The People of the Sea: A Journey in Search of the Seal Legends*. London: Arena. Legends of the selkies.

Whitehead, Ruth Holmes. 1988. *Stories from the Six Worlds: Micmac Legends*. Halifax: Nimbus. Legends of the Native Americans of Maine and Eastern Canada. The need for food and shelter is clearly of great importance in these stories.

Stories Related to Physics and Engineering

Allen, Pamela. 1983. *Who Sank the Boat?* New York: Coward, McCann. Fun with water displacement.

Brody, Ed, et al. 1992. *Spinning Tales, Weaving Hope*. See above. "Stubborn Turnip" deals with force.

Macaulay, David. 1975. *Pyramid*. Boston: Houghton Mifflin. Fascinating resource about the architecture and construction of the pyramids. The underpinnings for a great story.

———. 1977. *Castle*. Boston: Houghton Mifflin. The history and construction of a feudal castle.

———. 1988. *The Way Things Work*. Boston: Houghton Mifflin. A beautifully illustrated, encyclopedic book. Good resource for story facts.

There are many books by David Macaulay that give accurate and easy-to-understand information about design and engineering.

Valens, Evans G. 1958. *Me and Frumpet*. New York: Dutton. May be hard to find. It has an introduction by Edward Teller and its story deals with the physics of comparative size.

Stories Related to Science, History, and Biography

De Kruif, Paul H. 1932. *Microbe Hunters*. New York: Harcourt Brace. Wonderful stories to tell about great scientific discoveries and discoverers.

George, Jean Craighead. 1982. *Journey Inward*. New York: Dutton.

Stories Whose Protagonists Use Scientific Principles

Fox, Paula. 1966. *Maurice's Room*. New York: Macmillan. Maurice is a collector with endless curiosity and ingenuity. Read aloud or tell the stories.

Rockwell, Thomas. 1973. *How to Eat Fried Worms*. New York: Dell. Fun and funny. The hero solves his problem.

Sobel, Donald J. 1963. *Encyclopedia Brown* (series). New York: Bantam. Boy detective Encyclopedia Brown solves many mysteries by deduction and scientific knowledge. Lots of fun.

Thurber, James. 1943. *Many Moons*. New York: Harcourt Brace. A delightful fantasy about comparative sizes.

Ungerer, Tomi. 1971. *The Beast of M. Racine*. New York: Farrar, Straus and Giroux. M. Racine tries scientific methods and ends up taking his beast to great scientists to identify and classify.

Stories That Lead to Hands-on Experimentation

Allen, Pamela. 1983. *Who Sank the Boat?* New York: Coward, McCann. Water displacement and a mystery to solve.

Geisel, Theodor [Dr. Seuss]. 1949. *Bartholomew and the Oobleck*. New York: Random House. What *is* oobleck?

Greene, Melinda. 1978. *Bembleman's Bakery*. New York: Parents Magazine Press. A delicious story about the unique bread made by the seven Bembleman children.

Other Stories That Help Students Understand How Scientific Method Works

Almost any story is useful for this process. The only requirement is that students be encouraged to ask questions that take them beyond the story itself, and that the teacher be willing to follow where the questions lead. Examples in Chapter 3 and pages 73–76.

Stories About Counting

Anno, Mitsumaso. 1975. *Anno's Counting Book*. New York: Crowell. Beautifully illustrated with numbers and multiple objects to count (1–12) in each two-page picture. Includes a brief history of numbers.

Carle, E. 1969. *The Very Hungry Caterpillar*. New York: Putnam. Delightful, beautiful book, eaten by a very hungry caterpillar.

Gackenbach, D. 1981. *A Bag Full of Pups*. New York: Clarion. Counting to twelve.

Gag, Wanda. 1928. *Millions of Cats*. New York: Coward, McCann, and Geoghegan. Classic story about searching for one kitten. Very large numbers.

Friedman, Aileen. 1994. *The King's Commissioners*. New York: Scholastic. How to count to forty-seven in a number of ways. Grouping numbers. A delightful story.

Hutchins, Pat. 1982. *1 Hunter*. New York: Green Willow. Count to ten and back.

Stories About Pattern and Order

Burningham, John. 1980. *The Shopping Basket*. New York: Crowell. Delightful tale of Steven's shopping adventures.

Lippman, Peter. 1973. *Busy Wheels*. New York: Random House. Wheels of all sizes do the jobs that make our world go around.

MacAgy, Douglas, and Elizabeth MacAgy. 1959. *Going for a Walk with a Line*. New York: Doubleday. Patterns in art present new ways of looking at all sorts of things and seeing patterns.

Stories About Operations and Computation

Birch, David. 1988. *The King's Chessboard*. New York: Dial. One version of a traditional tale about the powers of two.

Eager, Edward. 1954. *Half Magic*. New York: Harcourt Brace. Children find a coin that gives them half of what they wish. Good for fraction practice.

Sagan, Carl. 1989. "The Secret of the Persian Chess Board." *Parade* magazine (February 5): 14–15. A discussion of the powers of two.

Stories Using Measurement

Aesop. 1968. *Aesop's Fables.* George Flyer Townsend, trans. "The Crow and the Pitcher." New York: Doubleday. A thirsty crow figures out a way to get the water within reach at the top of the pitcher.

Allen, Pamela. 1980. *Mr. Archimedes' Bath.* New York: Lothrop, Lee and Shepard. Amusing, illustrated, simple explanation. Mr. Archimedes in his bath with his animal friends.

Allen, Pamela. 1983. *Who Sank the Boat?* See *Stories Related to Physics and Engineering.*

Briggs, R. 1970. *Jim and the Beanstalk.* New York: Coward McCann. An updated retelling of Jack and the Beanstalk. Nice giant. Comparative size and measurement.

Hutchins, Pat. 1984. *Happy Birthday, Sam.* New York: Puffin. Picture book. A chair helps Sam to be big enough.

Krauss, Ruth. 1947. *The Growing Story.* New York: Harper and Brothers. Many ways to measure growth and change. Can also be used for science.

Swift, Jonathan. 1960. *Gulliver's Travels.* Boston: Houghton Mifflin. Classic. In this political satire, Gulliver visits the lands of the Lilliputians (tiny people) and the Brobdingnagians (giants). Comparative size.

Valens, E. G. 1958. *Me and Frumpet.* New York: Dutton. See *Stories Related to Physics and Engineering.*

Stories Using Time

Hutchins, Pat. 1970. *Clocks and More Clocks.* New York: Macmillan. Telling time.

Illen, M. 1956. *What Time Is It?* London: Routledge & Kegan Paul, Ltd. A children's history of time-keeping inventions and how they work.

Stories About Spatial Relationships

Anno, Mitsumaso. 1976. *The King's Flower.* New York: Philomel. A delightful story of a king who wants everything to be big enough to honor his importance.

———. 1989. *Anno's Math Games.* New York: Philomel. Different ways of thinking about many aspects of math. Includes cause and effect, patterns, perceptions, changes. Solutions and further thoughts for each chapter.

Hutchins, Pat. 1971. *Changes, Changes.* New York: Macmillan. Building with blocks. Changing shapes changes perceptions.

Books with Many Mathematical Ideas

Carroll, Lewis. 1981. *Alice in Wonderland*. New York: Bantam.
Lewis Carroll (pen name of Charles Lutwidge Dodgson) was a
mathematician and a delightful storyteller. Many applications.

———. 1981. *Through the Looking Glass*. New York: Bantam. The
sequel to *Alice*.

Juster, Norton. 1962. *The Phantom Tollbooth*. New York: Collins. Travel
with Milo to the lands of King Azzazz and the Mathemagician. A
great story filled with math and language ideas.

Teacher Resources for History

History is such a broad subject that I shall not attempt a content bibliography, with the exception of the three items that follow. Your history textbook, a good encyclopedia, appropriate biographies, well-
researched historical fiction of the period, and your librarian are all excellent resources.

Green, Roger Lancelyn. 1970. *Tales of Ancient Egypt*. See *Legends
and Myths*.

Kramer, Samuel Noah. 1981. *History Begins at Sumer*. Philadelphia:
University of Pennnsylvania Press. Translations from Sumerian
cuneiform tablets. Primary resource material.

Lipke, Barbara. 1993. "Bring History to Life with Storytelling."
Yarnspinner 17 (4): 1–3.

Stories for Multicultural Curricula

Carter, Angela. 1990. *Old Wives' Fairy Tale Book*. New York:
Pantheon. This collection has stories from many cultures and
features heroines. Some earthy.

Clark, Ella E. 1966. *Indian Legends from the Northern Rockies*. See
above.

Goss, Linda, and Marian E. Barnes, eds. 1989. *Talk That Talk: An
Anthology of Black American Storytelling*. New York: Simon and
Schuster/Touchstone. A comprehensive collection of stories
from Africa, the Middle Passage, slave times, and African
American culture.

Grimm, Brothers. 1963. *Grimm's Fairy Tales*. New York:
Macmillan. Probably western culture's best known collection
of fairy tales.

Hamilton, Virginia. 1985. *The People Could Fly*. New York: Knopf.
African American folktales.

———. 1988. *In the Beginning: Creation Stories from Around the World.* See *Legends and Myths.*

Lester, Julius. 1989. *How Many Spots Does a Leopard Have and Other Tales.* New York: Scholastic. A delightful collection of stories from Jewish and African American cultures.

Marriot, Alice, and Carol K. Rachlin. 1975. *Plains Indian Mythology.* New York: New American Library. An ethnographic collection of stories of Plains Native Americans.

Martin, Rafe. 1990. *The Hungry Tigress: Buddhist Legends and Jataka Tales.* Berkeley: Paralax. A generous and well-told collection of Buddhist legends, including the legends of Buddha's life.

Norman, Howard, ed. 1990. *Northern Tales: Traditional Stories of the Eskimo and Indian Peoples.* New York: Pantheon.

Reid, Bill, and Robert Bringhurst. 1984. *The Raven Steals the Light.* See *Legends and Myths.*

Sierra, Judy. 1992. *Cinderella.* Oryx Multicultural Folktale Series. Phoenix, AZ: Oryx Press. Twenty-five of the more than five hundred known versions of Cinderella, each with background information.

Singer, Isaac Bashevis. 1962. *Stories for Children.* New York: Farrar, Straus and Giroux. Jewish stories from eastern Europe, mostly Poland, including tales of Chelm, the town of fools, and many others.

Weinreich, Beatrice Silverman. 1988. *Yiddish Folk Tales.* Leonard Wolf, trans. New York: Pantheon. A large collection of classic Yiddish stories.

Yolen, Jane, ed. 1986. *Favorite Folktales from Around the World.* New York: Pantheon. A wonderful collection of tales arranged by type. Extensive bibliography and notes.

Zeitlin, Steven J., Amy J. Kotkin, and Holly Cutting Baker. 1982. *A Celebration of American Family Folklore.* New York: Pantheon. Family stories, true and apocryphal, arranged by type. How to find the stories in your family and get people to tell them.

Pantheon publishes collections of fairy tales and folktales of many countries.

Audio and Video Resources

Bruchac, Joe. 1990. "Gluskabe Stories." Cambridge, MA: Yellow Moon Press. An Abenaki Indian tells Native American stories.

Harley, Bill. 1986. "50 Ways to Fool Your Mother." Seekonk, MA: Round River Records.

———. 1987. "Cool in School: Tales from the Sixth Grade." Seekonk, MA: Round River Records.

———. 1988. "You're in Trouble." Seekonk, MA: Round River Records. Harley's stories and songs speak directly to kids.

Lipke, Barbara. 1995. "Tales from the Vineyard." Self-produced. Available from Yellow Moon Press, Cambridge, MA. Ghost stories and more. For older children and adults. Good for science questions.

Lipman, Doug. 1993. "Coaching Storytellers." West Somerville, MA: Enchanters Press. This video by a master coach demonstrates techniques that keep the storyteller feeling safe.

Martin, Rafe. 1994. "Rafe Martin Tells His Children's Books." Cambridge, MA: Yellow Moon Press.

O'Callahan, Jay. 1983. "Raspberries." Marshfield, MA: Artana.

———. 1984. "Earth Stories." Marshfield, MA: Artana. Parents' Choice Gold Award. Adventures of Herman and Marguerite.

———. 1985. "A Master Class in Storytelling." West Tisbury, MA: Vineyard Video Productions. A master storyteller tells his stories and gives tips on how to tell stories. O'Callahan has many storytelling tapes. His stories enchant all listeners.

This list is a small sample of the many audio and video storytelling tapes that are available commercially.

People Resources

Enright, Sheila. Mathematics Faculty, Newton Public Schools, Newton, MA.

Hereld, Katie. Storyteller. 857 Farmington Dr., Cheshire, CT 06410.

Hughes, Rita. Teacher and storyteller, Chester, CT.

Jacobson, Sara. Storyteller. P.O. Box 1489, N. Falmouth, MA 02556.

Lipke, Peter. Department of Biology, Hunter College, New York.

Naylor, Alice. Education Department, Appalachian State University, Boone, NC.

Ruane, Patricia. Superintendent, Needham Public Schools, Needham, MA.

Socia, Deb. 65 Pilgrim Ave., Fairhaven, MA 02719.

Stein, Fred. Education Director, The Exploratorium, San Francisco, CA.

References

Atwell, Nancie. 1987. *In the Middle*. Upper Montclair, NJ: Boynton/Cook.

Egan, Kieran. 1989. "Memory, Imagination and Learning: Collected by the Story." *Phi Delta Kappan* (February).

Hereld, Katie. 1993a. "Storytelling in the Math Classroom." Unpublished paper.

———. 1993b. "Storytelling in the Science Classroom." Unpublished paper. Both papers available from the address above.

Jacobson, Sara. 1993. "The Talking Stick." Workshop given at Sharing the Fire, Annual New England Storytelling Conference, Boston.

Schwartz, Marni. 1989. "Storytelling: A Way to Look Deeper." *English Journal* 78 (1): 42–46.

Socia, Deb. 1994. "Mathemagical Storytelling." Handout and annotated bibliography from workshop given at Sharing the Fire, Annual New England Storytelling Conference, Boston.

Usnick, Virginia. 1995. "Using Children's Literature in Middle School Mathematics." Handout from workshop given at the Annual Meeting of the National Council of Teachers of Math, Boston.

Wagler, Mark. 1994. "Jailbreak! Storytelling in Room 103." *Tales as Tools*. Jonesborough, TN: National Storytelling Press.